EDUCATION IN EAST GERMANY

World Education Series

General Editors: Michael D. Stephens,
 MA, MEd, PhD, FRGS
 Gordon W. Roderick,
 BSc, MA, PhD, MInst P

Education in
East Germany
(The German Democratic Republic)

MINA J. MOORE-RINVOLUCRI
Director, the Limerick Centre, Dept of Education,
University College, Cork

DAVID & CHARLES *Newton Abbot*
ARCHON BOOKS *Hamden, Connecticut*
1973

For Bernard and Brenda

This edition first published in 1973 in Great Britain by
David & Charles (Holdings) Limited, Newton Abbot, Devon
and in the United States by Archon Books, Hamden,
Connecticut, 06514

ISBN 0 7153 5969 X (Great Britain)
ISBN 0 208 01339 3 (United States)

Set in eleven on thirteen point Imprint
and printed in Great Britain
by Latimer Trend & Company Ltd Plymouth

Contents

5

Foreword

THERE are two main obstacles to the study of East German education for the English-speaking student: one is the dearth of material available in his own tongue and the other the insistent repetition and interweaving of unfamiliar politically conscious theory with educational issues and development that is characteristic of work published in the German Democratic Republic. It is this latter feature that causes many educators west of the Elbe, often lacking first-hand experience of the system, to doubt the value of its educational claims and to query its effectiveness after only twenty-eight years of existence.

Frequent study visits made to the country in recent years, consultations with ministry officials, regional and local directors of education, professors, lecturers, researchers, principals of colleges and schools, teachers, students in training and children, together with access to the relevant documentation, have made it possible for me to attempt to bridge a gap. Seeing the system at work in all types of educational institution, I have been able to evaluate it objectively, in terms of its own claims.

To the Ministry of Education of the GDR who supplied material and to the numberless German people who made this study possible, I would like to express my deep gratitude.

M.J.M-R.

Regions of the GDR, with chief towns

I

Some Aspects of the GDR

EXTENT AND POPULATION

THE German Democratic Republic, with a surface area of 41,380 square miles, was in 1945 the Soviet zone of occupation and made up of five states (*Länder*): Brandenburg, Mecklenburg, Saxony, Saxony-Anhalt and Thuringia. It declared its independence of Federal Germany on 7 October 1949. In 1952 the five states were fused and the country was divided into fourteen administrative regions (*Bezirke*) with East Berlin, the capital, forming a fifteenth. In each case the chief town gives its name to the region.

The big cities have population counts as follows:[1]

City	No of inhabitants
East Berlin	1,083,173
Dresden	503,726
Karl-Marx-Stadt	297,133
Magdeburg	268,000
Halle	261,190
Leipzig	258,904
Erfurt	193,997
Rostock	193,699
Gera	111,188
Potsdam	110,949
Schwerin	94,453
Cottbus	80,329
Frankfurt/Oder	60,365
Neubrandenburg	41,612
Suhl	30,945

The above list read in conjunction with the figures below gives some idea of the relative densities of population, the heaviest being in the industrial south:

Region	No of inhabitants
Karl-Marx-Stadt	2,057,200
Halle	1,930,890
Dresden	1,877,131
Leipzig	1,496,432
Magdeburg	1,320,588
Erfurt	1,255,822
Potsdam	1,133,631
East Berlin	1,083,856
Cottbus	857,353
Rostock	856,224
Gera	737,748
Frankfurt/Oder	677,119
Neubrandenburg	639,582
Schwerin	598,041
Suhl	552,887

The total population today is 17,074,504: 7,851,573 males and 9,222,931 females.

Much has been made in Western Europe of the population drain to the Federal Republic, stemmed in 1961 by the demarcation of the frontier (in Berlin, the Wall). Little is heard of the steady flow, admittedly of lesser proportions, from West to East Germany. The German Democratic Republic is not an overcrowded country (157 persons to the square kilometre) but it is a land rich in history and the custodian of a great cultural heritage.

SOCIALISM IN OPERATION

When the Soviet Union was in command in 1945, the land was nationalised and the junkers and big landowners were expropriated without compensation. The land was transferred to those who worked on it, most of whom eventually combined in collective farms, the rest preferring to cultivate small-holdings. At the same time, banking and big business were also nationalised.

On the creation of the GDR,[2] power was transferred to workers and peasants. The country is a member of the Warsaw Pact and of the Council for Mutual Economic Aid among members of the Socialist bloc, but Soviet soldiers are today little in evidence and the GDR has become a country in its own right. As an industrial power it ranks fifth in Europe (after the Soviet Union, Federal Germany, Great Britain and France) and ninth in the world. It has slender mineral resources (brown coal, lignite and potash) but is thickly wooded. Its main industries are machine construction, chemicals, precision engineering and the production of optical instruments, electrical and electronic engineering, and agriculture.

Collective farms represent the cultivation of 86 per cent of the total arable land; the remaining 14 per cent is made up of small-holdings and market gardens. The chief crops are wheat, rye, potatoes, sugar-beet, hay, hemp and oil seed. Pasture land is in the north.

GOVERNMENT

Politically, all power is vested in the People's House (for which the age of qualification is twenty-one, though the age of majority is eighteen) which is composed of 500 members,[3] men and women, elected by secret ballot on the basis of universal suffrage.

The Council of State, elected by the People's House, is responsible for putting the decisions of that assembly into operation. Walter Ulbricht was chairman of both Houses and Head of State (the office of President having been abolished in 1960) until 1971 when he resigned in favour of Erich Honecker. The People's House also elects the thirty-eight members of the Council of Ministers, the executive organ of both the House and the Council of State.

The main political parties have united to form the Socialist Unity Party with the newspaper *Neues Deutschland* as its mouthpiece.

The first Constitution was worked out in 1949; the second, the one operative today, in 1968.

The regions are administratively subdivided into 26 urban districts, 191 rural districts and 9,055 municipalities and communes (*Gemeinde*).

RELIGION

The total separation of church and state in this largely Protestant part of Germany, the land of Luther, made the private sector in education a thing of the past. Church land was not nationalised in 1945, and religion, keeping to its own spiritual domain and to corporal works of mercy, is not persecuted.

In the census of 1964, 10,091,907 people, that is 59 per cent of the nation, declared themselves adherents of the various Evangelical churches (mainly Lutheran) in some 7,800 parishes with 6,000 ministers. 1,375,237, that is 8 per cent of the nation, declared themselves Roman Catholics. Of these, 4,100 were members of religious orders: the 1,400 men were mainly Dominicans and Franciscans, the 2,700 women were Benedictines, Franciscans, Ursulines, and Sisters of St Elizabeth.

The exact number of Jews in the eight autonomous communities, the sad remnant of the days of terror, is not recorded. New synagogues[4] were built for them in Erfurt, Karl-Marx-Stadt and Magdeburg. In other places damaged synagogues were restored.

Yearly government grants are made to both Protestant and Catholic churches and can be used for rebuilding, repairs, or charitable purposes; and these grants are supplemented by church collections and by authorised public collections, run by recognised bodies for charitable purposes. There are departments of Protestant theology in all the universities and study there, like all other study, is financed by the state. Catholic students for the priesthood are trained in the seminary at Erfurt. People are not excluded from office by reason of their religious beliefs. If they can accept the social doctrine as compatible with their beliefs, and play their full part in society, they have the same rights and

duties as all other citizens. But there may well be points of conflict where the individual has difficulty in reconciling a humanist
point of view with his own religious convictions, and few children can be expected to be strong enough to stand out from the
majority of their classmates. It is admitted that the percentage of
churchgoers in the upper classes of schools is on the decrease,
though the churches still remain full.

The state is concerned with political and social life, with, as
it were, life on earth: religion, as such, has no part to play in
school and college. In this, the condition of GDR children does
not differ from that of children in the public sector of USA
education, or, indeed, of French education. They receive religious instruction in their churches, where a weekday timetable
for all children of each age group, taught separately, is publicly
announced week by week at every church service.

SPORT

The outstanding performance of the GDR in the world of sport
is in part accounted for by the emphasis placed, at all levels, on
the importance of physical culture. It is taken very seriously,
linked with health education, and viewed as something very desirable in its own right as well as of importance to mental growth.
Sports facilities, among them stadiums, gymnasiums, swimming
baths, sports centres and clubs, are available for the whole
population.

Notes to this chapter are on p 118

2

Historical Retrospect

THE SOVIET UNION AND GERMANY

FOR an examination of East German education as we know it today it is not necessary to go back further than 1945.[1] The part of Germany that was allotted to the Soviet Union as its zone of influence at the end of World War II was in one sense the fruit of victory. It was inevitable that a deep revulsion should be felt by the Soviet Union for the invaders who had carried on the war so fiercely on Russian soil. The 900 Days of Leningrad, for example, constituted an experience not shared by the USA or Great Britain. This made it harder for her to view the possible resurgence of Germany with anything but dread and she was uncompromisingly determined to prevent such a danger to herself.[2] From the German side, thirteen years of nazi propaganda had convinced most Germans that communism was an entirely repugnant philosophy. There could have been deadlock between conqueror and conquered and there were certainly difficulties, some of which were to flare up in 1953.

YALTA AND THE CONTROL COMMISSION

The Crimea Conference Communiqué issued after the meeting of Churchill, Roosevelt and Stalin in Yalta (3–11 February 1945) —the collapse of Germany being then only a matter of time—had finalised the agreement to divide Germany into three zones of occupation, or four if France accepted the invitation to 'participate as fourth member of the Control Commission'. Among its avowed intentions was that of removing all nazi and militaristic influences from public offices and from the cultural life of the German people.

> It is our inflexible purpose to destroy German militarism and nazism and to ensure that Germany will never again be able to disturb the peace of the world. We are determined to disarm and disband all German armed forces, break up for all time the German General Staff that has repeatedly contrived the resurgence of German militarism; remove or destroy all German military equipment; eliminate or control all German industry that could be used for military production; bring all war criminals to justice and swift punishment and exact reparation in kind for the destruction wrought by Germans; wipe out the nazi party, nazi laws, organisations and institutions; remove all nazi and militaristic influences from public offices and from the cultural and economic life of the German people; and take in harmony such other measures in Germany as may be necessary to the future peace and safety of the world.
>
> It is not our purpose to destroy the people of Germany, but only when nazism and militarism have been extirpated will there be hope for decent life for Germans and a place for them in the comity of nations ...[3]

The total surrender of Germany to the Allied Forces ended the 1939–45 war in Europe. On 2 May the Russians entered Berlin. The four victorious powers, Britain, France, the USA and the USSR, delegated their authority to a Control Commission, in a statement signed jointly by General D. Eisenhower, Lieutenant-General G. E. H. Robertson (deputising for Field Marshal B. L. Montgomery), General L. Koeltz (deputising for General P. Koenig), and Marshal G. Zhukov. The official Gazette of the Control Commission for Germany (no 1 appeared on 29 October 1945) gives in four languages the various proclamations, laws and directives put out by the Allies.

All armed forces, associations and clubs serving to keep alive the military tradition in Germany were disbanded and in Gazette no 11 the word 'militarist' is defined as anyone who (i) seeks to bring the life of the German people into line with a policy of

B

militaristic force, (ii) advocates or is responsible for the domina-
tion of foreign peoples, their exploitation or displacement, (iii)
for those purposes promotes armaments.

Germans were recalled from the countries they had invaded;
money and foreign assets were frozen. Shipping was immobilised
and Allied control over public services, though these were run
by the Germans themselves, was made clear; the law and the
police force were to be reformed and war criminals brought to
trial. In the liquidation of everything nazi, teacher, student and
youth organisations were included; and all textbooks were to be
destroyed, except for library samples for scholars.

The whole layout of these documents, which also deal with
reparations, reflects the unease and the striving for precedence
that existed among the Allies. The Gazette (see p 17) was
arranged in parallel columns. The first number begins with
Russian in column 1: in subsequent issues French and English
take their turn in column 1 and it is stressed that German,
always in column 4, appears only by courtesy. Russians, in their
own dealings with Germans, always issued their orders in
German and it is worthwhile noting that twenty-six years later,
the USA ambassador to West Germany, Kenneth Rush, is
stated to have been prepared to sign the Four-Power Pact on
Berlin only if agreement were reached on a German language
version. To the one produced the GDR raised objections on the
grounds of misinterpretation and the question was left open.[4]

THE POTSDAM CONFERENCE

From 17–25 July and 26 July–2 August 1945 the Tripartite
Conference of Berlin took place at the Cecilienhof, Potsdam,
and was attended by Churchill, Attlee, Stalin and Truman in
session one, and by Attlee, Bevin, Stalin and Truman in session
two. They produced the document known as the Potsdam Agreement, which decided, among other things, that as far as practi-
cable there should be uniformity of treatment of the German
population throughout Germany and that economically Germany

should be treated as one.[5] The following clauses alone have a bearing on education:

6   All members of the nazi party who have been more than nominal participants in its activities to be removed from public and semi-public office and from positions of responsibility in important private undertakings. Such persons shall be replaced by persons who, by their political and moral qualities, are deemed capable of assisting in genuine democratic institutions in Germany.

7   German education shall be so controlled as completely to eliminate nazi and militarist doctrines and to make possible the successful development of democratic ideas.

CONTROL COUNCIL DIRECTIVE 1947

On 25 June 1947, Directive no 54 of the Control Council (that is, of the four Allies) listed a number of approved principles and transmitted them to zone commanders and to the Allied Military Command in Berlin, not as of obligation, but for guidance:[6]

1   There should be equal educational opportunity for all.

2   Tuition, textbooks and other necessary scholastic material should be provided free of charge in all educational institutions fully supported by public funds which cater mainly for pupils of compulsory school age; in addition, maintenance grants should be made to those who need aid. In all other educational institutions, including universities, tuition, textbooks and necessary material should be provided free of charge together with maintenance grants for those in need of assistance.

3   Compulsory full-time school attendance should be required for all between the ages of six and at least fifteen; and thereafter, for those pupils not enrolled in full-time educational institutions, at least part-time compulsory attendance up to the completed age of eighteen years.

4   Schools for compulsory school attendance should form a comprehensive educational system. The terms 'elementary education' and 'secondary education' should mean two consecutive levels of education, not two types or qualities of instruction which overlap.

5   All schools should lay emphasis upon education for civic re-

sponsibility and a democratic way of life, by means of the content
of the curriculum, textbooks and materials of instruction and by
the organisation of the school itself.

6   School curricula should aim to promote understanding of and
respect for other nations, and to this end attention should be
given to the study of modern languages, without preference for
any language.

7   Educational and vocational guidance should be provided for
all pupils and students.

8   Health supervision should be provided for all pupils and
students. Instruction should also be given in hygiene.

9   All teacher education should take place in a university or a
pedagogical institute of university rank.

10 Full provision should be made for effective participation of
the people in the reform and organisation as well as in the administration of education.

Done at Berlin, 25 June 1947.

This document, which Conant the American educationalist
described as the best expression of a democratic system of education, came two years after the Soviet zone had got education well
under way. Moreover, the Russian interpretation of the word
'democratic' and the expression 'participation of the people' were
bound to lead to differences in practice. The Soviet zone took the
words of the Potsdam agreement seriously.

COMMUNISM GOES INTO ACTION

It may well be that the preparedness of the Soviet Union for the
stages after total surrender gave them an advantage in their own
zone over Western Germany where Allied opinion was divided.
They had experience in building up schools in a socialist society,
and they insisted on their own set of values; these factors played
a major part in the setting up of the scientifically based education which bears its fruits in the GDR today. But Soviet plans
were not made alone. In 1944, the German Communist Party
working underground with the support of an organisation of
Free Germans in the Soviet Union was dedicated to the over-
throw of Hitler. They had set up a working party of twenty

members under Wilhelm Pieck to make a post-war educational scheme for Germany, and they were ready to put a ten-point plan forward at the conclusion of hostilities.[7] This plan was meant to be for the whole of Germany. On 11 June 1945 the German Communist Party addressed an appeal to the German people to prevent a repetition of the mistakes of 1918. It seemed to them that after twelve years of nazi control of the lives and thoughts of German youth, the concomitant of necessary social change was inevitably the abolition of the class-character of educational structures, the cultivation of the spirit of peace and respect for all men, and the harnessing of all young people to a totally different ideology. The Allied victory was seen as giving an opportunity for a new, forward-looking type of education. It is the contention of the GDR that their ideas on education could have been adopted for the whole of Germany had there not been so much discussion about political reform, autonomy of the separate states, retention of confessional schools and the preservation of middle-class values. The plan was refused countenance by the Western powers, among whom there was divided thinking about the means of implementing the Potsdam Agreement. It could, therefore, become operative only in the Soviet zone. But it is important to stress that there was a basic plan for Germans, made by Germans, before the total surrender.[8]

SOVIET ORDER OF AUGUST 1945

The Soviet Military Authority's Order no 40 of 25 August 1945 was, for its zone, the opening of a new educational era.

In order to prepare for the work of the schools in the territory of the Soviet Zone of Occupation in Germany, we hereby order

I. The Director of the German Central Administration for national education, the district councils, the mayors of the towns and regions of the Soviet Zone of Occupation

a. to make sure, in preparing the schools for work, that measures are taken to ensure a complete liberation of instruction and education from nazi, militaristic, race and other reactionary theories as well as from all elements of theoretical and practical pre-military training;

b. to arrange for setting up education in the elementary, secondary (upper schools, *Aufbauschulen*, gymnasiums), technical schools and colleges; the school year in all general and technical schools to begin on 1 October of the present year;

c. to convert all private schools at national, provincial, area and district level and to hand them over to the control of the territorial and local authorities; the opening of any general education or technical private school is forbidden;

d. to work out syllabuses for the schools and submit them for ratification to the Soviet Military Administration in Germany through the Director of the German Central Administration for national education by 15 September 1945;

e. to forbid the use of textbooks, in all subjects, which were published in the period of the fascist regime and contain nazi, militaristic and racial theories; these books to be taken from schoolchildren and the responsibility for this confiscation to be delegated to the school managers and teachers;

f. to prepare textbooks for printing, for which purpose the textbooks published prior to 1933 are to be utilised and submitted for approval to the Soviet Military Administration in Germany: for the elementary schools by 10 September and for secondary schools by 1 October of this year;

g. to give out lists of recommendations of School Literature published before 1933 and to submit them for approval to the Soviet Military Administration by 15 September of this year;

h. to register all teachers who were formerly employed in the schools and to take on those of them who took no active part in fascist organisations and societies and who are qualified to carry out democratic principles in the teaching and educating of the children and to unmask the reactionary nature of nazism, the racial theory and the military character of the former German State;

i. to approach such persons from among democratic, anti-fascist circles of the German intelligentsia who have had the necessary all-round education and want to be employed as teachers in elementary and secondary schools, in educational work.

II. The Commanders of the Soviet national, provincial, area and district commands are ordered

a. to exercise control over the activity of the local German autonomy in the area of elementary education;

b. to examine and approve: schools, principals and teachers; the heads of the territorial and local elementary education departments; plans for out-of-school activities for youth and children.[9]

In pursuance of this order Russian organisation worked at speed and in co-operation with teachers, on the first $3\frac{1}{2}$ million textbooks for the reopened schools (see p 26).

THE TEACHING FORCE

In the Soviet zone in 1945 the average age of teachers, excluding those of Mecklenburg, was fifty-two years, and in Berlin fifty-nine. Many teachers had been killed, gone into exile or been taken as prisoners of war. If the schools were to be utterly different from the traditional German school, the need for younger teachers to operate new ideas was a priority; only about 20 per cent of all teachers were kept on and not all of these on a permanent basis.

There were some teachers who had fallen foul of the National Socialists and lost their posts between 1933 and 1945; others had contrived to avoid involvement. Consequently, so long as these men and women were prepared to accept the new conditions, their services could be retained, but a huge new teaching force had to be created. Some 40,000 were needed. And so arose the unparalleled situation of an emergency training of an almost total teaching force, all volunteers, accepting in the main socialist ideas, people from all walks of life, and without experience of schools other than those which they had attended as pupils. The first cohort received minimum ad hoc training by German teachers and Soviet educational personnel not yet demobilised. Armed with a provisional syllabus, in the indescribable chaos of post-war Germany they took over classes. It was an uphill task in every way. A sense of vocation or a desire or willingness to

build up socialism were no substitute for knowledge. Some
parents, and indeed some children, found it difficult to accept
the idea of common schools in the hands of working people and
their sympathisers, most of them sketchily trained into the bar-
gain; and men who were once in this position honestly admit that
there was opposition to them and hostility to what they stood
for. And that opposition may have taken some colour from
awareness that the educational situation in the Soviet zone and
that prevailing at the founding of the USSR were very different
indeed. Germany had no illiteracy problem, no backward population; there was a long tradition of good teaching, considerable
educational expertise and organisational ability.

These hurriedly trained men and women came to be known as
the New Teachers. One such man, today the headmaster of a
large polytechnical secondary school in Rostock, relates that he
had never stood in front of a class before and was only a page or
two ahead of the pupils he had to teach. Another, today a professor in the pedagogical institute in Potsdam, became a headmaster
at eighteen. It is understandable that the Western zones were
scornful of these early teachers in the Soviet zone, and retrained
any who fled there.

The need to raise a big teaching force was intensified by the
great influx of children from the German territories under Polish
control. The *Täglische Rundschau*, the paper of the Soviet Administration, said pertinently on 13 December 1945: 'One could
write excellent textbooks, work out great syllabuses and find progressive methods of instruction but it would be a waste of time if
there were no teachers capable of putting them into practice.'

So the earliest New Teachers, working in schools in the daytime, went on with crash courses in the evenings, at weekends,
in the holidays. They had to go into class with each lesson written
out in full, and they not only had to work very hard over lesson
preparation but also to effect their own political education. They
had, it is true, directives about lesson-content and general
method, but they had to fight their way against pupils who had

been brought up to regard Communism as essentially evil. Inevitably, most opposition to the new schools was at secondary level where the hard facts had to be learned that no one section of the population could have privileges for the buying, that denominational schools had gone, and that religion had no place in a humanist orientated school.

In 1945–6 some 1,500 teachers were receiving a fuller training on an eight-months' course and in 1946–7 some 2,500. Those of the first hurried hour subsequently retrained to become fully qualified teachers, but while they waited their turn a commission worked out detailed monthly assignments for them.

Without waiting for schools to function and immediately after the war, the Soviet military authorities had encouraged people who felt concern about the plight of children in rubble-strewn towns to group them together informally, give them jobs to do, and teach what was possible.

The first schools were reopened in July and all 22,000 by 18 October 1945. The schools were to be totally comprehensive, open to all children without distinction of social origins, home background or location. They were to be of one type only, with basic schooling from six to fourteen years,[10] entirely free, the classes mixed and unstreamed. Urban and rural schools were to be placed on equal footing with equal education of a purely lay character. They were to place emphasis on good working habits and on ready service to the community.

1946 LAW ON THE DEMOCRATISATION OF GERMAN SCHOOLS

All these provisions were legislated for, along with the equal right of every child to education as far up the educational ladder as it could go, in the 1946 Law on the Democratisation of German Schools. The GDR contends that this law marked a new era in German education in that it was education without exclusivity, education for all people, without in any way repudiating or seeking to minimise Germany's past contribution to world education from Luther to Francke, Froebel and Diesterweg. It is repeatedly emphasised that grammar and intermediate schools had been middle-class schools to which a working-man, whether in town or country, could not afford to send his children, either in terms of money or déclassement. It is further contended that while the rest of Germany quarrelled to maintain the status quo, here was a new, just conception of education, egalitarian and not, as the Western powers maintained, merely the sovietisation of their schools.[11]

SOME PROBLEMS AND DEVELOPMENTS

One-class schools One of the early organisational problems of education tackled in the zone was that of the closing down of one-class schools, of which, immediately after the war, there were 4,114, or 40·7 per cent of all schools. This figure was reduced to 23·7 per cent in 1946; in 1948, there were still 1,407 such schools; then came the Rural School Reform in 1955 and that year there remained only 55 one-class schools in the GDR as against 8,054 in Western Germany. In the GDR today there are none, thanks to the creation of central schools for children of ten and over, either accessible by school bus or with boarding facilities. The improved educational facilities for country children initially met with opposition until it became evident that their education would not drain them away from the land.

Textbooks Order no 70, 25 September 1945, caused the creation of the state publishing firm, the Volk u. Wissen Verlag, which had already, without official existence, been helped in July 1945, in terms of allocation of paper and provision of transport etc, to produce the first schoolbooks on Weimar models. These first books were not ideal, nor were they even geared to the emergent new school. By the end of 1945, 4,116,000 books had been produced. After 1949 more German research guidance became available about textbooks and other educational requirements, for in that year the German Central Pedagogical Institute—since September 1970 the German Academy of Pedagogical Sciences—was founded to research into and give guidance on all educational matters.

School, home and community The theory of Comenius that education must be a partnership between the school, the home and the community has been made effective. The first Parents' Associations were formed in 1951 and a work element (in field, factory or business) of 10–12 hours a week was incorporated into the education of all young people in February 1946 (this has since been substantially reduced). But the one-type comprehensive school of today, the polytechnical secondary school, with no alternatives, is the realisation of an ideal formulated in 1956, subsequently reinforced, logically worked out, and not abandoned as it has been in the Soviet Union.[12] Polytechnical education does not go in for a vague kind of handwork but makes a real and vital contribution to production, and gives a science-based initiation in a range of jobs and trades, without, however, being a substitute for apprenticeship.

In 1956 at the Third All Party Congress compulsory general education became the rule, with full secondary education seen as compressible into two years. This latter conception has been modified. The speeding up of the primary stage of education to increase time for secondary subjects was only made generally effective in the Soviet Union in 1970 and then only for mathematics and Russian. But in the GDR it was first worked out in 1961 and, stage by stage, made operative in all subjects, a year at a time, as from 1965, with the progressive production of new, attractive textbooks to meet new situations and with new methodology to make their use fully effective.

In 1968 new-type citizenship courses were introduced in the top classes of all schools and in the same year plans for a new conception of vocational education were put into force.

EXPERIMENTATION

The GDR has today compulsory re-training schemes for all teachers and has become a nation wholly committed to—and well in advance of many others—the process of continuous learning. Educational ideas proliferate and are utilised with a thoroughness characteristic of the German people. When allied with the drive of socialist thinking, the result of all this is a non-static, well-integrated and efficient system.

The school is conceived of as an environment conducive to the growth of teacher and taught. Its relations with the community are made effective by the involvement of parents, trade unions and youth movement, and by the link between classroom learning and actual, not simulated, productive work. It is a fruitful attempt to close the gap between learning and living. And it is for all. Regardless of their origins, children can get the fullest education of which they are capable, physically, mentally and morally. And, from the outset thought was given to society's need of people and people's need of society, and also to what has only latterly engaged the attention of some Western nations, the condition of the deprived and hitherto under-privileged child.[13]

Under the first two-year plan of 1949–51 changes were gradual since hope of the unification of all Germany was still alive. The five-year plan of 1951–5 moved faster and ushered in bigger programmes of experimentation. Naturally enough the GDR is kept, partly by other nations' policy of non-recognition but mainly by a shared ideology, in close contact with educational thought in the Soviet Union and exchanges research findings with that state. Is this vastly different from the proliferation of American-conceived ideas which rouse interest and sometimes enthusiastic acceptance in other countries, as for instance the plan to introduce a system of educational credits in Federal Germany in 1971?

Notes to this chapter are on p 119

3

The educational system and pre-school provision

STRUCTURE OF THE SYSTEM

IN studying the education of countries which have a written constitution, it is well to be aware of those sections of it which are specifically concerned with the subject in hand. The constitution of 1968 contains the following clauses:

Article 17 1. Science and research as well as the application of their findings are essential foundations of socialist society and are fostered by the state in every respect.
2. The GDR assures to all citizens a high standard of education corresponding to the constantly increasing social requirements through the integrated socialist educational system. Citizens are thus enabled to shape socialist society and to participate creatively in the development of socialist democracy.
3. The GDR promotes science and education with the aim of protecting and enriching society and the life of the citizens, of mastering the scientific technical revolution as well as of guaranteeing the constant progress of socialist society.

Article 25 1. Every citizen of the GDR has an equal right to education. Educational facilities are open to all. The integrated socialist education system guarantees every citizen a continuous socialist education, training and higher training.
2. The GDR ensures the march forward of the people to a socialist community of universally educated and harmoniously developed men and women imbued with the spirit of socialist

patriotism and internationalism and possessing an advanced general and specialised education.

3. All citizens have the right to participate in cultural life. Under the conditions of the scientific-technical revolution and increasing intellectual demands this becomes of growing significance. The state and society encourage the participation of citizens in cultural life, physical culture and sport for the complete expression of the socialist personality and for the growing fulfilment of cultural interests and needs.

4. In the GDR attendance at the general ten-year polytechnical secondary school is compulsory. In certain cases secondary schooling may be completed within the framework of vocational training or further education of workers. All young people have the right and duty to learn a vocation.

5. Special schools and training establishments are provided for mentally and physically handicapped children and adults.

6. The carrying out of these tasks is ensured by the state and all socialist forces in joint educational work.

Article 26 1. The state ensures the possibility of transference from one stage of education to the next up to the highest educational institutions, the universities and colleges; this is done according to performance, social requirements and consideration of the social structure of the population.

2. There are no tuition fees. Training allowances and free study materials are granted according to need.

3. Full-time students at the universities, colleges and technical schools are exempted from tuition fees. Grants and allowances are given according to need and academic prowess.[1]

The Ministry of Education is located in Berlin. The Minister of Education, always a teacher and presently a woman, Margot Honecker (also the wife of the new Chairman of the House), is elected, or re-elected, for a period of two years. She is advised by a Secretary of State, four Deputy Ministers and an Educational Council.

In each region (*Bezirk*) there is an education office and a Subject Commission to which the best teachers are elected by the authorities to help the rest to utilise new methods and to understand and put into practice new educational ideals, translating into classroom usage new approaches and methods. This work is mainly done in seminars, held in the Teachers' Club (see p 102).

In the regional office there is a director of education, three assistant directors, five inspectors and an education committee. Each region is divided into local authorities with a director and two inspectors. It is the work of both the regional and local authorities to ensure that ministry directives are carried through. A similar responsibility is incumbent on headmasters and headmistresses, who are responsible for all teachers in their schools, politically and educationally; they deal with inefficiency, recommend for courses and eventually, in consultation with the local director, for promotion.

The whole education system is structured in such a way that it is closely knit from kindergarten to tertiary level. Children of working mothers can be looked after in a nursery until they reach the age of three, then the kindergarten, which is still outside the limits of compulsory schooling, caters for the child from three to six. The years of compulsory schooling are from six (seventh year of age) to sixteen in the one-type polytechnical secondary school. Children who are physically or mentally handicapped are in special schools. From the age of ten children unusually gifted at sport or music get more intensive training in these areas, without abandoning their general all-round education: their day is merely prolonged and very demanding. When the ten-year schooling is over and crowned by a leaving examination, it can be followed by further courses:

1. A further two years in an extended secondary school—the work is virtually begun with children of proven academic ability in years nine and ten of the polytechnical secondary school, a provision that will no longer be made when the raising of the general level of the polytechnical secondary school warrants it. The intensification in classes nine and ten is a matter of longer hours and a heavier syllabus, the pupils here taking the ten-year leaving certificate and also after twelve years the *Reifeprüfung*

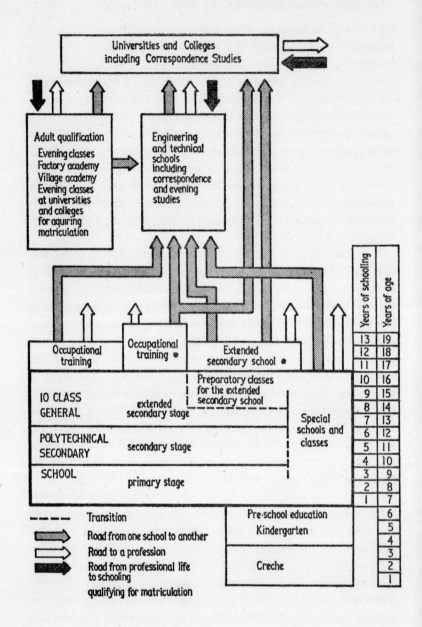

(*Abitur*) corresponding in a measure to English A levels—but no longer the trade certificate (see p 56).

2. A two-year period in a vocational school, ending with the twelve-year leaving certificate, the *Abitur* and a trade qualification.

3. A one-year period in a vocational school.

Once the purely formal period of study is concluded, that does not necessarily mean the end as far as education is concerned. At any age up to thirty-five a person can begin where he left off and climb up the educational ladder through evening classes, correspondence courses and part-time courses (which are in any case compulsory for those who leave school before eighteen).

PRE-SCHOOL INSTITUTIONS

Young babies and children to the age of three can be looked after at a crèche during the working day. A student, a teacher and any working woman gets official free time to come in to attend to the physical needs of her baby and is free of the gnawing anxiety that grips so many students and working women, especially those without relatives, in some other countries. The crèche, often part of a factory complex and always a gay and happy place, is in the charge of a nurse and a team of helpers, the whole thing state-licensed and controlled.

The kindergarten is not part of compulsory education, catering as it does for the pre-school child from the age of three to the age of six, but it is state-supervised and run by trained people. Some are set up by firms or farms and some by the city or rural council. One of the reasons for their existence is that the economy, making no unequal distinctions between men and women, needs the work, whole or part-time, of as many women as possible. Work is arranged so that a man and wife are never on the same shift, and one of the parents can be responsible for taking the child to kindergarten or school and the other for collecting him at the end of the day. Shops forming part of the factory complex facilitate the buying of household necessitites, and men and

c

women share domestic duties. It has also long been recognised that equality of opportunity at the start of formal education is vastly helped by giving more children the opportunity for the enrichment of play and untrammelled development at an earlier age. The routine and group activities help children to mature and their minds to develop; speech is stimulated by the hearing and use of a wider vocabulary than some homes can provide, and a happy environment with games and unrestricted movement is conducive to mental and physical growth.

All the kindergarten buildings I have seen in the Democratic Republic were modern, airy, light and well supplied with indoor and outdoor play material of all kinds: an adventure playground, sand, slides, swings out of doors, and indoors a very high standard of cleanliness. The kindergartens are often divided up, so that each age-group has its own washing facilities and its picture-labelled possessions opposite its own gay classroom. There is great emphasis on hygiene, on beauty in the environment and on the informal learning absorbed from pleasant surroundings. Toys, live animals—holidays and weekends constitute no hazards to the life of pets since the kindergarten is always near the houses where the children live—plants, flowers, paints, construction sets, toys, plasticine, water, action songs, dance, story-sessions, all make for reading- and number-readiness, though so far there is no formal learning. There seems, however, less free expression, less uncontrolled experimentation in painting than, say, in English nursery schools.

Children who spend full days rather than mornings in the kindergarten are cared for by trained assistants in the afternoons, taken for walks, encouraged to observe and to talk. Some kindergartens take children as weekly boarders, others are ready to keep them for longer than the ordinary daytime hours. Table manners and courtesy are cultivated, and the degree of precision in carrying out little tasks and the children's attitudes to such tasks are not only a delight to observe but are also invaluable in laying the foundation of good orderly habits for work and living.

I came across one exception to the general rule of no formal education and that was in a kindergarten in Halle; it affected immigrant Greek children. In order that these children, whose fathers work on building sites or in factories, should not through living in exile lose their own national patrimony, they were being taught to read in Greek and were spoken to in Greek, but only on two mornings a week, that is for one-third of their kindergarten time. On the other four days and often out at play they used German and were not found confusing the languages (this ability of a young child to keep separate two linguistic areas is not unusual). Their bilingual teacher, a Greek by nationality and the mother of five children, who was studying to qualify in her spare time, created such a gay and happy atmosphere that well-integrated development was possible.

In Federal Germany there are fewer kindergartens per head of the child population, but these in the GDR are provided from district or factory funds and employees are ready to mend toys, lay out grounds, and make contributions to provide materials which the children need. Occasionally a kindergarten is actually on a factory site, although the teachers are not factory employees but are paid by the state.

Children who do not spend three years in a kindergarten are encouraged to attend one in their last pre-main school year, even if only on a part-time basis, in order that they too can be made school-ready and prepared for living in the school community.

The latest in nursery school building is to be seen in Halle-Neustadt, a vast complex built outside Halle for workers in the chemical plants. It is a circular building set round an inside playground and has an interesting undulating roof-line using recently developed delta (Greek d-shaped and curved) tiles to cover the convex roof.

Notes to this chapter are on p 120

4
Polytechnical Education

THE NATURE OF POLYTECHNICAL EDUCATION

POLYTECHNICAL education could be superficially described as a science-based education geared to life in a technological age and appropriate to a national system born at a time when technology was moving very fast. It could be said to aim at a high level of scientific instruction in all school subjects that engage hand and head; its theory is tested out in real-life situations, which means that young people are expected to work in factory or business as part of their general education.

That it makes great demands on teachers and children is unquestionable, and there has in fact been a reduction of time spent in factories to meet the contention that older children had no time for themselves. Until 1970 the leaving-certificate candidate had at the end of his twelve-year schooling to take in addition a trade certificate; this has been abrogated to alleviate strain and pressure.

Polytechnical education is designed to close the gap between those who think and those who do, in a world that calls increasingly for a skilled and intelligent work force. The basis of instruction is mathematics and natural sciences in their theoretical aspects and practical application, with other subjects catering for aesthetic, artistic, physiological and emotional development. There is great emphasis on the mother tongue as a tool for the acquisition of knowledge and for personal enrichment, and on the study of at least one foreign language.

36

In the GDR every child, while still at school, gets multi-sided practical experience of the working world in farm or factory, workshop or business concern, and learns to respect the jobs of all men who work efficiently. This is basic to the whole of a child's school life and increases in importance as the child moves up the school. Included in the conception of polytechnical education is the conviction that school is more than a threshold to life in a grown-up context: it is part of that life. The work done in school is seen as a contribution to the life of the community and the community has serious collective and personal obligations to the school. In the awareness of this, in the effort it calls forth and in the satisfaction of a duty fulfilled, the individual finds his fulfilment in an entity much bigger than himself and develops his personality and potential to the full.

COMPULSORY EDUCATION

The years from six to thirteen are those of compulsory schooling, begun after the child attains the age of six, and carried out in one-type schools, in which the youngest children are in class 1 and the oldest in class 10. The first three years are devoted to work of a primary nature, the next three to intermediate studies and the last four to secondary schooling.

The total number of ten-year polytechnical secondary schools is 6,923: they are found in the regions as follows:

Berlin	173
Rostock	468
Schwerin	372
Potsdam	567
Neubrandenburg	560
Frankfurt/Oder	381
Cottbus	380
Magdeburg	563
Halle	675
Erfurt	520
Gera	314
Suhl	261

Dresden   592
Leipzig   427
Karl-Marx-Stadt   670

The buildings are sometimes the solidly built secondary schools
of pre-war days, repaired and adapted. The new purpose-built
ones, often with a central staircase, spacious halls, a gymnasium,
even their own swimming bath, are well planned, light, full of
plants, flowers, pictures and trophies won by individual pupils
and teams.

In order that there be no 'join', and as there is no moving
from one type of school to another and no privileged form of
education, the one name 'polytechnical secondary school' is used.
No child is excluded from learning the secondary range of
subjects, so that no child can leave school feeling that he did not
have a chance. His teachers all have a trade as well as their
teaching qualification: the child from class 7 (age thirteen) forwards learns his basic skills alongside men who make their living
by them. At the appropriate age he is made aware of the significance of his skills in the economy of the country, of the costing of production processes, and of each man's responsibility to
all other men.

In school the class is, overall, taught as a unit, seated in single
desks in front of the teacher, except in the science laboratories
where children work at benches for three, on each side of a row
of sinks which extend from the front to the back of the room.
In workshop practice the work is often individual. What is most
heartening to a teacher from England is the total absence of the
depressing attitude sometimes encountered in his own country
and summed up in the words: 'They can't do it: it's a waste of
time teaching them.' And precisely because GDR teachers do
believe in the children and make a determined effort to help
them, even the less gifted make a positive response. The norms,
centrally set, are high. It is the responsibility of the headmaster
or headmistress to see that these norms are reached, that children who need it get extra help from a class tutor (a kind of

auxiliary but fully trained teacher), and that teachers plan and do their work well. Children are taught by classteachers during their first three years at school and then by specialists. Syllabuses for each subject and each level and handbooks of suggestions are issued, centrally produced. There is one textbook for each subject for each year and its contents are the year's assignment for that subject. This is the minimum that all must acquire but it is not designed to limit the teaching nor to cramp the style of the good teacher. Able teachers write or collaborate in writing textbooks. There is no dearth of supplies. The headmaster of one very large school has introduced the idea of having a complete set of the ten textbooks in the subject taught in the subject room kept on a ledge under each child's desk. The appropriate one for the year is for daily use, the others are for consultation as need arises. At home each child keeps a duplicate of the books in use in his year, so obviating the need to carry a heavy bag of books daily between school and home.

Children are taught in unstreamed classes averaging 27·7 per class (1969). They attend school only in the morning, on six days a week, and normally from 8 am to 1 pm; they have homework on only four days: Monday, Tuesday, Thursday and Friday. There are whole-day schools where there is a call for them, for example where parents cannot provide adequate supervision of their children in the afternoon, or where children with learning difficulties can be helped by a tutor to keep pace with the other children in their age group. The whole-day school can be an enriching experience for children who may need wider opportunities than their homes can provide.

In accordance with German custom, lessons are *taught*: the children do little written work in class-time; the full session is used for exchange between teacher and class and the atmosphere is one of industry.

From the timetable on p 40 one can see that there is total equality of opportunity for all children in all subjects offered by the school. All get a chance to see how they fare with each subject.

Timetable for the school year 1971-2

Subject	Class 1 1H*	Class 1 2H*	2	3	4	5	6	7	8	9	10
German	11	10	12	14	14	7	6	5	4	3	3
Russian	—	5	6	6	—	6	5	3	3	3	3
Maths	5	5	6	6	6	6	6	6	4	5	4
Physics	—	—	—	—	—	—	3	2	2	3	3
Astronomy	—	—	—	—	—	—	—	—	—	1	1
Chemistry	—	—	—	—	—	2	—	2	4	2	2
Biology	—	—	—	—	2	2	2	2	1	1	2
Handwork	1	1	1	2	1	—	—	—	—	—	—
Gardening	—	—	—	1	1	—	—	—	—	—	—
Polytechnical instruction, made up of:											
Introduction to socialist production	—	—	—	—	—	—	—	4	4	5	5
Technical drawing	—	—	—	—	—	—	—	1	1	—	—
Production work	—	—	—	—	—	—	—	—	2	2	3
History	—	—	—	—	—	2	2	2	2	3	3
Civics	—	—	—	—	—	—	—	1	1	1	2
Drawing	1	1	1	1	1	1	2	1	1	1	—
Music	1	1	1	1	1	1	1	2	1	1	—
Physical training	2	2	2	2	3	3	3	2	2	2	2
Number of hours per week	21	21	24	27	29	31	33	32	32	31	32
Needlework (optional)	—	—	—	—	1	1	—	—	—	—	—
Second foreign language (optional)	—	—	—	—	—	—	—	3	3	3	2/3
TOTAL	21	21	24	27	30	32	33	35	35	34	34/35

*H = half-year

A wise feature of the timetable is the distribution of science subjects in such a way that no subject takes up so many periods as effectively to preclude the learning of the others. So every single child gets the fundamentals in each science, and none of the sciences so spread out across the timetable is without its modicum of utility even for those children whose lack of ability make it unlikely that they will use it in earning a living. At least they help to make sense of life in the twentieth century, and no child will later look back on his schooldays and say that because he was never given the opportunity he does not know what chemistry, for example, is about. Nor (except in German, mathematics and Russian) does any child see stretching before him the quite dismaying prospect of five or so periods a week devoted to a subject that does not engage his full and enthusiastic attention! The total, however, together with physical education, music and drawing, adds up to a general all-round education, the prerogative of all children.

The intensive cultivation of the mother tongue at all levels, with a spoken, reading and written command of it, is regarded as an indispensable tool in education, a feature shared with most advanced countries. So is, increasingly, the teaching of what might be termed, and what ought to be, the universal language of the twentieth century, mathematics, with its emphasis on mathematical thinking and expression. Its importance is here attested by its time allocation.

THE FIRST THREE YEARS (AGES SIX TO NINE)

The content of the centrally planned syllabuses for the whole country was set out in a law of 1965, in so far as the lower level of the school was concerned, as:

1. Instruction in German and in its oral and written use.

2. Mathematics: with all that is implied in the term 'new mathematics', leading to the development of abstract thinking.

3. Simple manual training and gardening instruction; elementary instruction in technical, technological and economic matters;

simple technical drawing and work skills; a survey of the
economy of the home region.

4. Singing, music, drawing, painting and modelling.

5. Sports instruction and all-round basic physical education.[1]

To sweep one difficulty from the path of first-year children a
simplified script approximating more closely to print was introduced in 1968. The elaborate curves and flourishes of German
handwriting take much effort to produce at an age when motor-
controls are not fully established, and the time spent on them can
be more fruitfully used. The new script uses printed capitals
and simplified small letters, which can eventually become more
elaborate and more characteristically German, as the child moves
up the school.

In the lower part of the school (classes 1–3) a greater condensa-
tion and intensification of content have been introduced in order
to get basic things done more quickly and more efficiently. This
has been a gradual process, worked out since 1964, level by level,
a year at a time, with new syllabuses, new textbooks and new
teaching aids. By putting four years' work into three more can
be done in the middle school (classes 4–8) and in the upper
school (classes 9 and 10). But the gradual implementing of this
decision to increase the content of the syllabus was a measure
wisely conceived and worked out with considerable care. It is
interesting to note that the USSR implemented a similar intensification, in Russian and mathematics alone, in 1970.

Any big changes in approach and method are worked out in
specially designated experimental schools where able teachers and
researchers co-operate to measure degrees of success or failure
of new ideas. Successful experiments, once validated, pass into
general use. New mathematics is taught right from the outset,
so that the child learns to form mathematical concepts and to
speak mathematically.

The manual work of the lower and most of the middle school
is done in paper, plastics, straw, leather and wood, with a
striving for standard and finish which will make the work saleable.

Gardening is seriously undertaken: not the sporadic cultivation of personal plots but the care of a big kitchen garden growing vegetables for the school or even the factory canteen, under the supervision of a gardener. It is designed to be run as an economic proposition and costs, sales and profits are seriously worked out.

CLASSES FOUR TO TEN (AGES NINE TO SIXTEEN)

Although in the last seven years of compulsory schooling the terms intermediate and secondary appear to draw distinctions, these years form a bloc.

By the age of twelve, when the mother tongue could be judged to be rooted in the child's mental processes, comes the obligation for every child to learn a foreign language. This is naturally Russian, since relations with the USSR are important and also because egress to other countries is very much limited by West Berlin's control of travelling permits.

The official requirements for the ages nine to eleven are stated as:

1. German language and literature.

2. Mathematics, ensuring the consolidation of fundamental principles and the practical application of mathematical knowledge to problems in natural science and in practical work.

3. Natural science subjects taught in classroom, laboratory and in the field.

4. Manual training and school garden instruction including teaching of simple technical and agrobiological matter.

5. Social science instruction including historical and political knowledge.

6. Foreign language instruction: emphasis on oral methods in the learning of Russian.

7. Singing, music, drawing, painting and modelling.

8. Sports instruction: continuation of basic physical training; increasing use of sports competitions; allowance to be made for different interests and inclinations in out-of-school sport.

9. Polytechnical instruction appropriate to the age of the pupils and geared to job opportunities in the area.

At the upper or secondary level, where techniques of independent work are to be consolidated, the following things are required:

1. Mathematics: introduction to mathematical analysis, geometry, and simple applied mathematics.

2. Natural sciences (physics, astronomy, chemistry, biology and physical geography): fundamental facts, scientific laws, methods and procedures, together with a study of the long-range importance of the natural sciences and their role in production.

3. Polytechnical instruction: systematic teaching of the scientific-technical, technological and political-economic foundations of socialist production; use of modern machines, installations and devices; development of socialist attitudes towards labour through close contact with teams of working people and through the independent responsible carrying out of production tasks.

4. Social science instruction: acquiring of basic historical and political knowledge; application of this to present-day problems; instruction in civics and introduction to economic, philosophical and political bases of Marxism-Leninism.

5. German: oral and written expression to be further perfected; acquaintance with humanist works of the past and present; recognition of nature of socialist realism; outside reading to be encouraged.

6. Foreign language: in addition to Russian a second foreign language is optional in classes 9 and 10 (ages fifteen and sixteen) and this, as a rule, is English; pupils to be able to make themselves understood in the foreign languages, to read and understand simple texts of a general and popular scientific content and to gain an understanding of other nations.

7. Sports instruction: high norms of performance; pupils to acquire the sports badge and the most talented the olympiad badge.[2]

LAYOUT OF SYLLABUSES.

It would be interesting to present a whole range of detailed syllabuses but to do so would require a volume of encyclopaedic proportions. Perhaps a very small sample may serve as an indication. Let us look first at year two in German. The year's work is divided into thirty-two weekly assignments, each an amplification of the themes dictated by the compulsory textbook: traffic, houses today, parents at work, the seasons, the station, postal services, the army, life of children in other lands—to make a random selection. These themes appear in column one. In column two is listed compulsory and complementary reading; column three suggests exercises in calligraphy related to the theme of the week; column four deals with dictation and spelling, column five with grammar, column six with oral and written self-expression. These indications take up only 10 pages; the other 154 are devoted to suggestions for each lesson, the difficulties, the illustrations to be found by the teacher, and teaching aids appropriate to each week's work. There is no chance for any teacher to run out of ideas and every chance that his own thinking will be stimulated.

For English and Russian the syllabus is based on TV courses viewed in the child's own home or in the home of a classmate. Re-viewing is possible since the same programme is repeated each week; the textbook used in class is the TV script. The textbooks of even eight years ago, with their prejudiced views of France and England, are no longer used.[3]

In the biology syllabus, for each theme there are facts to be mastered and practical observation to be made. The humanist approach is very much in evidence and man is viewed solely in his development as a member of the animal kingdom. For practical work there are biology rooms with aquaria, plants, small live animals, and stuffed animals as good as those owned by museums. Children are taken on excursions and on visits to biological stations, and have to do as much fieldwork as the area allows.

The civics syllabus is concerned with the bases of scientific socialism, socialist ethics and morality, duty to the community and contributions to its welfare. It is political in outlook and ethical in content.

AN INTEGRATED CURRICULUM

As the subjects stand on the official timetable, they may present no little similarity with those of official timetables in many other countries. But these subjects are not separately conceived and studied in isolation; they are looked on as part of a wider whole and make an integrated curriculum through which runs the guiding thread of the polytechnical idea. For years a team at the Polytechnical Institute of the University of Halle, under the guidance of Professor H. Wolffgramm, has done remarkable work on the methodology of polytechnical education and the whole question of scientific integration, not only in terms of the present but taking into account likely demands and developments up to the end of the century. No doubt this is why the GDR has not felt a need to abandon the concept of polytechnical education as the Soviet Union has done.

Every child gets a chance to do, indeed has to do, manual work in classes 1–6, and in classes 7–10 he goes to work for one day in each week in a factory, a works, a centre which is in effect a simulated factory, or a business. This outside work is done in groups if there are more than twenty-one children in the class and is so arranged that children get experience in more than one section of a plant, with an eight-week period of easing in and then real involvement in production. They are moreover taught several processes so that head and hand are educated and job choices are widened, a very useful provision in an increasingly automated society.

When polytechnical education was first launched in a big way, the reaction of some parents, especially of professional parents, was one of perplexity, not unmixed with a degree of anxiety. Some were anxious for their daughters plunged into factory life and some feared lest polytechnical education might diminish the chance of subsequent entry into a profession. The attitude of pupils was mixed, but boys, especially, welcomed the new idea. Today it is better understood, better integrated into the syllabus and more readily accepted. The factory or farm service which the children share with their teachers and those whose occupations lie there is much more real and valuable to them than, for instance, metalwork done in school conditions, and it has been found that girls take to tools and machines in a most amazing way. In rural schools the children get agricultural experience and learn about crop cultivation, improvement of fruit production, dairy farming and produce, and, where appropriate, the uses of wool, hide, horn and feather. In all cases there is discussion of markets and of the problems of the farming community, especially in relation to the implementation of the various five-year plans for agriculture and the advantages and disadvantages of collective and co-operative farming.

Whether the children work in factory or farm, their poly-technical schoolteachers accompany them (many have themselves worked in the enterprise) but the actual initiation into the practical work is given by one of the workers, often elderly, with some teacher training and a love of his trade.

One of the best examples of a factory training centre, one of many in the GDR, is in Berlin-Friedrichshagen. The layout is that of a factory making rotary mowers, windscreen wipers and television parts. Here the director was once a workman and trained as a teacher by correspondence courses. A workman gives an introductory talk to class seven about what is required on their production day: arrival before 7.30 am, clocking in, serious atti-tudes to work, care of machines, safety precautions (teachers can be tried in court and lose their jobs if accidents happen while they are supervising works practice). Each pupil in the course of the year is initiated into each of the stages in the production of an article and learns to respect tools and machines. He is given a change of job every month, not only to improve his skills but to help maintain his interest. He is also taught about inspection procedures, giving consideration to possible improvements, reduction of costs, increase of profits. To my observation that the pupil gets more variety than ever he will find in a factory where he is chained to one process came the answer: 'If he is aware of this it is up to him to get factory conditions changed.'

Does this mean that all children will automatically go to the trade to which the location and resources of their school have assigned them? They are under no compulsion to do so, but since their work-training, be it in electronics or the production of machine tools or chemicals, has got them some distance on the road to a trade, many do find jobs in that trade. However, the work done over four years in the polytechnical secondary school is not vocational, as the Minister of Education stressed at the seventh Pedagogical Congress in 1970, but is intended to be a link between learning and day-to-day life, and a unifying principle in the curriculum, a way of developing in children a love of work, a sense of punctuality, responsibility, economy and mutual helpfulness.

SPECIALIST SCHOOLS AND CLASSES

This one-class society has no élitist escapes. Specialist schools on the scale known in the USSR (where there are special opportunities in English, French, German, Spanish and other language schools for children of seven and a half and upwards) are few and reserved for those German children who can take all their education in Russian, or for those who are outstanding at sports and are willing from the age of ten to accept the discipline of a 7.30 am to 5 pm day, grafting intensified sport on to general education, or for those talented enough to make music a career.[4] It is, however, noteworthy that the children of officers in the Russian garrison do not attend the Russian schools for German children; they have their own camp schools. (Below the rank of officer men do not have their families with them.) There are *no* English or French schools. In the main, pupils in specialist schools envisage the *Abitur* at the end of their school life, but not necessarily so for people who are highly gifted in music or sport and destined to become performers.[5]

There is some thought of creating specialist *classes*, not schools, for art, mathematics/science and technical subjects, but the present intention of the GDR is not to let these classes multiply unduly and it insists on everyone having works training in order to maintain solidarity with the community. Another deviation from the idea of the same ten-year school for everyone is for those who show special aptitude by the end of year eight and can look forward in all likelihood to carrying on through the extended secondary course in years eleven and twelve. They have certain extras added to their timetable in years nine and ten, to match their ability.

Similarly, children who, because of their modest degree of mental capacity or by reason of insuperable physical or mental handicap, have really reached their ceiling after eight years of schooling can then take jobs, usually unskilled, and attend part-time vocational instruction for two years. An all-out drive will in time be made to devise ways of keeping them fruitfully in full-time schooling till sixteen, so that the word unskilled may eventually drop out of the GDR vocabulary.

By whatever road he travels, at whatever speed he climbs the ladder, the door to tertiary education is never de facto closed until the individual reaches the age of thirty-five. Correspondence courses, evening classes and pre-university preparation give people who regret having left school too soon a chance to re-train, to add to their qualifications, to reach more ambitious goals.

RECORDS

Every school has a visitors' book in which signatures, and occasionally impressions, can be recorded. This is usually a very handsome volume kept in the headmaster's room and reserved to visitors of note.

Most schools have a log-book, an illustrated diary of school

D

events, to which a foreign visitor may contribute pictures of his homeland. And each class has a journal (as in West Berlin schools) which gives an account of work done and marks given, comments included, and is signed by the teachers.

For every child from the age of six the school keeps a personal report book with twenty-three double pages, the twentieth section marking the end of compulsory schooling. Half-yearly the cumulative mark, averaged, for each subject is entered by the teacher in the child's report book on a five-point scale: 1 very good; 2 good; 3 satisfactory; 4 passable; 5 unsatisfactory. There are in addition evaluations of personal qualities, a general assessment, an indication of promotion chances and remarks about conduct, orderliness and co-operativeness. Absences are recorded, and this half-yearly report is signed by the class-teacher and the headmaster. When the twentieth section is reached the book is also stamped by the competent educational authority. By the end of school life the book constitutes a continuous assessment of work, character and service to the community. Inside the cover of the book is a space for recording honours and special distinctions.

There is no corporal punishment, detention or punitive extra homework. Sanctions are censure of one who lets the class down, entry in the class journal, reports to the headmaster and misdemeanours entered on the cumulative report or threat of transfer to another school. In extreme cases the child is referred to the probation services. In classes 10 and 11 there can be expulsion from the school, which means no further direct study, though after a period of twelve months application can be made for a further education course. If an entry has been made in the pupil's report book it can be cancelled by a year's good behaviour. On the final certificates no punishment record is ever entered, so that no young person is haunted by his escapades or lapses.

When a child leaves school he receives from the headmaster, who presides over the ceremony, his *Abschlusszeugnis*, his ten-year leaving certificate. This registers his final subject marks, his achievement in productive work, machine technology or, if appropriate, plant cultivation and animal husbandry, as well as his introduction to socialist production. In the case of languages, mention is always made of the number of years of study. The certificate is signed by the examination commission and with it the young person can be sure of finding work immediately though this is not the only possibility open to him (see p 53).

EQUIPMENT AND COMMUNITY SUPPORT

Much thought has been given to the provision of subject rooms in schools: this means not only science and language laboratories (the latter are in the main sonorised classrooms) but rooms where the equipment, illustrative material and so on, pertaining to each subject, are collected. This 'localisation' of each subject is valued by teachers and pupils alike.

At first the equipment for programmed learning, devices operated by the pupil to flash his answer to the teacher, were made in the school, built, fitted and serviced by the teachers themselves. Equipment, especially electrical and electronic, was already of a very advanced nature in 1965: electrically controlled black-boards, advanced storage devices, elaborate illustrated and illuminated wall charts to integrate literature, biology, art and music, and an abundance of electrical microscopes. The *Interscola* section of the Leipzig Fair today exhibits a very wide range of school furniture and educational equipment from the GDR as well as from Sweden and other exhibiting countries. Now, with central supplies and loan services the whole pool of equipment available to all schools has been vastly enlarged. Indeed, much research is currently being carried on in the GDR on the subject of audio-visual aids and, on a world-wide scale, on the installation and equipment of subject rooms.

As pupils in a school are expected to know the world of work, so the world of work is expected to know the schools; and this means not only the parents but people in general, who as members of society must take an interest in schools. The whole community is expected to be interested in their own school and to serve the needs of the young people in it, mainly with voluntary labour—for example, in repairing furniture or laying out grounds—but also in discussing their own jobs and perhaps using their specialised knowledge to help individual children. Moreover every school has a patron, be it factory, plant, enterprise, business concern, ship or farm. The employees are expected to be interested in 'their' school. Sometimes highly qualified chemists or engineers may supplement the teaching in the schools and are very highly respected as 'doers'.

When the Ernst Thälmann Polytechnical Secondary School in Erfurt was built in 1961–2, at a cost of 900,000M, people gave their services to help with the construction to the value of 100,000M. In Halle-Neustadt the radio and weather stations were built without public funds, and school gardens were laid out by various citizens who had no direct connection with the chemical industry for whose workers the town was created.

This bringing together of administrative personnel, teachers, tutors, parents and politicians to take corporate responsibility for the welfare of all children is a feature of socialist education and has a double function, that of giving real support to the child in his formative years and that of minimising the risk of deviant tendencies. The conception of the school collective means that everyone who works in any capacity in the school—head, teachers, tutors, pupils and all auxiliaries, including cleaners—works as a member of a team which is expected to have the interests of the whole at heart. Consequently, a lapse in standards or a lack of responsibility on the part of anyone is letting down the side and deserves careful scrutiny. This idea of the collective is of course not confined to schools but is found throughout society in the GDR.

Notes to this chapter are on p 120

5
Beyond Compulsory Schooling

THE EXTENDED SECONDARY SCHOOL

AFTER the completion of the ten-year school a child has a better chance of making choices. The most academically able, about 13 per cent of the school population, follow the two-year course in the EOS (*Erweiterte Oberschule*) of which there are 304 in the Republic, distributed in 1969 in the regions as follows:

Berlin	13
Rostock	15
Neubrandenburg	13
Schwerin	13
Potsdam	24
Frankfurt	15
Cottbus	18
Magdeburg	25
Halle	33
Erfurt	24
Gera	17
Suhl	12
Dresden	24
Leipzig	26
Karl-Marx-Stadt	32

They accounted for a total of 51,923 boys and girls with an average of 25 in a class.

What selection criteria are used for admission? First, every pupil has taken his ten-year leaving certificate and made very good progress as evinced by his cumulative report. The second

Timetable for the extended secondary school 1970–2 (see p 56)

Subject	System till 1970					1971–2	
Classes:	11	I2				11	12
		A	B	C	K		
German	3	4	4	4	4	3	3
Russian	3	3	3	3	3	3	3
Second foreign language	2	4	3	4	4	2	5
Third foreign language	—	5	—	7	—	—	—
Mathematics	5	3	4	3	4	5	5
Physics	3	1	3	3	3	3	3
Astronomy	—	1	1	1	1	—	1
Chemistry	2	1	3	1	3	2	3
Biology	2	2	2	—	2	2	3
Geography	2	—	1	—	—	2	—
History	3	3	3	3	3	3	—
Civics	1	1	1	1	1	1	2
Sport	2	2	2	2	2	2	2
Art	—	1	1	1	1	—	—
Music	—	1	1	1	1	—	—
	28	32	32	32	32	28	30
Compulsory elective subject:							
Scientific/practical work	4	—	—	—	—	4	4
Art or music	1	—	—	—	—	1	1
Elective up to	33	32	32	32	32	33	35
	3	—	—	—	—	3	1
Total hours a week up to	36	32	32	32	32	36	36

criterion is that during the trial years in classes 9 and 10, he has fulfilled the hopes placed in him. Originally the two years of the extended secondary school were a self-contained addition to the ten-year general school, a kind of 'higher top'. Now they are prepared for in classes 9 and 10 by a slight redistribution of time and a loading of syllabuses for which a marked degree of stamina is required, the ordinary syllabuses for these classes themselves being of an exacting enough nature. When the whole school population achieves a full ten years' schooling—the obviously less able are at present allowed to drop out after eight years— the special timetables in classes 9 and 10 for the more able will be discontinued, because the 'coaching' element now involved in them will no longer be necessary. At present parents can ask for their children to be admitted to these special preparatory classes but the decision rests with the headmaster, the class tutor and teachers, together with the headmaster of the extended secondary school, the local education authority having the final say.

The third criterion of selection is performance in the olympiads, the school-work competitions. These are inter-class, inter-school, inter-city, national competitions, in several rounds, in mathematics and the sciences, and now even in foreign languages and German. The olympiad is useful for stimulating work in given areas and for focusing the attention of researchers, scientists and professors on the most highly gifted so that eventually they can be given teaching commensurate with their abilities and have the opportunity of reaching their full potential. This very high-powered teaching for pupils who have proved their ability to study, and their capacity for intensive work, and who have those qualities of character that make a good research worker, can be had in five special extended secondary schools. All of them are mixed boarding schools, boys on one floor and girls on another, with private rooms and studies that compare more than favourably with those provided by the biggest English public schools. The boarding fees are minimal and maintenance grants generous.

Most of the pupils go home at the weekends and have 75 per cent of the fare paid.

In every extended secondary school the pupil works for his final leaving certificate, the *Abitur* (*Reifeprüfung*), and spends increased time in production. Up to 1970, along with the *Abitur* he was obliged to get a Work Certificate. That has now been abolished in this sector, but the work for it has not.

Heretofore in classes 9, 10, 11 and 12 the pupil worked to an all-round syllabus with special emphasis on one aspect. In 1969 the number of compulsory hours was reduced from 36 to 28 for general subjects with a larger time allowance for the area in which the pupil showed greater interest and aptitude. These areas are shown in the table on p 54, where A = modern languages, B = mathematics and natural sciences, C = classical languages, and K = combined syllabuses. Four hours practical work is undertaken each week in a factory or other enterprise in furtherance of the polytechnical ideal.

Since 1970 there has been a series of options: social science, a third foreign language, extra mathematics and science, probability calculation, mathematical foundations of computer technology, physics of solid bodies, macro-molecular chemistry or ecology. They have catered for more tastes, but increased the time spent in class.

The schools can be highly experimental. Thus in the Carl Schorlemer School in Merseburg, a lecture/private-study/seminar technique has been tried out under the direction of the professor of physics in the University of Halle, and there are analogous experiments in other places to improve methods of study and promote greater efficiency and independence of working at a later stage. Yet there is also a certain amount of anxious thought about the advisability of using methods usually associated with the more mature university student.

Another very interesting school is the EOS boarding school of Schulpforte, between Naumberg and Kösen. It was originally a Cistercian foundation and was secularised at the time of the

Reformation when it became first a court academy with a modified classical and Christian education and later a gymnasium. After 1945 it was brought into the mainstream of education and had to admit all comers, mostly, but not exclusively, from rural areas round Halle. Today it has 340 pupils, both boys and girls, within the age range of fourteen to eighteen and a teaching staff of twenty-three. The boarding fee is 45M a month and there are grants according to need, free laundry and subsidies for holiday activities. Interestingly, this school has not only obligatory Russian but also, for almost all those who attend it, obligatory Latin. Its political and sports activities are the same as those of other schools; its links with production are rural. It is an amazing fusion of old and new. The list of past pupils is a proud one and includes the names of the musician J. H. Scheen, the philologist Ernest, the writers Schlegel and Klopstock, the philosophers Fichte and Nietzsche, the mathematician Möbius, and Bettman Hollweg the chancellor of the Reich from 1909 to 1917, besides many scientists, scholars and men of letters. It has a modern observatory, and an amazing library of 45,000 bound volumes and 40,000 paperbacks and pamphlets; it has medieval manuscripts and vellum-bound editions of the Fathers, treasures from the days of the Cistercians, *incunabula*, autograph letters of many of its distinguished past pupils, and many, many first editions, as for example of Herder's works. It is, in short, a great research library for scholars from all over the world yet it is also used by the boys in the school.

Many of the monastery buildings are preserved, and constitute a historical monument alongside the very modern classrooms of the school today.

In all schools, whether polytechnical secondary or extended secondary, there are clubs in all the main school subjects, where keen pupils can pursue their knowledge further. There are also recreational activities for all tastes, from sport to dramatics, from choir to model train construction and, in country places, beekeeping.

THE VOCATIONAL OR OCCUPATIONAL SCHOOL

The second road to further educational opportunity is the one-year vocational school which continues general education, combining it with some instruction in a particular trade. From here a boy can take a semi-skilled job and work upwards by study in evening classes or by correspondence courses that relate to the work he does in the daytime but prepare him for promotion.

The third road is the two-year vocational school, training for a specific trade. This course embodies a very large element of practical work so that when the boy or girl has completed it and got his *Facharbeiter Schluss* (specialist leaving certificate) it is equivalent to having served an apprenticeship. In the course he spends two days of seven hours in the classroom, engaged in general study and on the theory of his specialisation, and four days a week in the workshop, learning complementary trades. He emerges a middle-range technician, able to go on to an engineering or a technical school to become a highly skilled engineer or technician.

The fourth road is the three-year course at a vocational school, ending with a work certificate and the *Abitur* which secures admission to any tertiary level establishment.

Vocational or occupational education of all the types enumerated above is given in 400 schools under the State Department for Vocational and Occupational Education (*Berufsausbildung*). The practical part of the work, done in factories, business concerns and farms, has been made the direct responsibility of those accepting trainees, according to norms laid down at national and local level. The objective is to diminish the numbers of people untrained for a job and to increase the numbers of skilled workers that can be absorbed into the economy.

The nation has given much attention since 1968 to this sector of vocational education, raising the general level and making the standing of the school really comparable with that of the extended

Timetable for the training of a wireless mechanic

Subject	Instruction half-years					
	1	2	3	4	5	
1. Theoretical vocational education						
Electrotechnics/electronics	8	6	6	6	—	Theory in years 1 and 2
Diagram reading and making	1	1	1	—	—	38 weeks per year
Mathematics	1	1	—	—	—	
Science of materials	1	1	—	—	—	Practice in years 1 and 2
Economics of job	—	—	2	2	—	38 weeks per year
Basics of BMSR-technics	—	2	2	1	—	
Basics of electronic data work	—	—	—	3	—	In addition 10 weeks full practice
2. General education						
Civics	1	1	1	1	—	
Sport	2	2	2	2	—	In year 3 (1st half)
Hours per week	14	14	14	15	—	21 weeks full practice
Days per week	2	2	2	2	—	
3. Practical work						
Practical work including connecting, testing, marketing	26¼	26¼	26¼	26¼	43¾	
Days per week	3	3	3	3	5	

secondary school in public esteem. Young people not only learn
how to do a job, or a complex of jobs; they learn the maths and
science and economics involved, and make a study of health and
safety regulations in factories. Part of the training is devoted to
the discussion of standards in industry and labour conditions, to
instruction in civics, and to physical education. Full mastery of
a particular job is achieved by doing a piece of personal work
under the supervision of a master craftsman and on the most
up-to-date lines; and not only is the student required to work at
one trade but at technically related trades, and, in the interest of
his own future, is made to think out how those trades will adapt
to increased automation. Students are encouraged to show initiative, and importance is attached to any suggestions and criticisms
they may have to offer.

Only good factories and businesses, with high standards, are
used for practical work. The pupil is invited to participate fully
in factory meetings concerned with quality of work, lowering of
costs and raising efficiency of personnel. The use of good
forward-looking enterprises is deliberate, to avoid perpetuating
obsolete working methods. Some boys and girls, of course, want
to be apprenticed to crafts, to artisan-type work, to privately
owned concerns or small businesses. This is allowed, so long as
the theory can be covered in a school.

THE FACTORY VOCATIONAL SCHOOL

There is yet another way to full qualification for an occupation
and that is via the factory vocational school (*Betriebsberufschule*).
There are some 705 of these, and the education given here has,
since 1969-70, been made chargeable to the factory though the
teachers are paid by the state. These schools function at all levels
of education (see chapters 4 and 5, pp 43 and 53) and the
Ministries of Education and of Technology are both concerned
in the safeguarding of standards and conditions.

Some of these schools, part of the factory complex, are very
large indeed. In the chemical works Leuna I (Halle), the factory

school has 115,000 pupils under instruction at various levels, and 486 teachers. There are three sections in the school:

1. The polytechnical eight-year school, which will eventually be phased out. From here come the semi-skilled workers.

2. The polytechnical ten-year secondary school. From here come skilled workers, foremen and technicians (with suitable vocational training).

3. The extended secondary school where the teachers are supplemented by the firm's engineers and scientists, whom the pupils can see working in the factory. From here come future top-ranking engineers and scientists, with tertiary level qualifications.

Such firms provide classrooms and laboratories, chemicals, equipment, and work instructors; and they use in the factory the metal work, spare parts and machine tools made by the pupils from class 7 on. All technical subjects are taught by specialists with shop-floor experience, or by men with first-hand knowledge of costing, marketing and the business side of the enterprise.[1]

Because of the wide range of work in a big factory and because the pupil in the factory school 'belongs' in a special way, the school does provide a potential pool of labour and a high degree of job-security, though without exerting pressures on the boy or girl who wants to go elsewhere.

THE THRESHOLD OF THE WORKING WORLD

The whole subject of vocational education was thrashed out by factories, educationists, apprentices themselves, and the general public before the Law for the Further Development of Vocational Education, 11 June 1968, made it part of the comprehensive educational system—and a very important part, affecting the lives of 440,000 apprentices and their choice of 1 of 450 possible trades. Research workers in the GDR contend that of these 450, 50 are basic; and there will be progressively more grouping of them, so that combinations of subjects can be offered. An apprentice needs to learn more trades than one in the area of his interest, in order to understand how the business works and what part he himself is to play in its economy and running. He needs to have a good overall view of modern technology and an awareness of human relationships if he is to derive satisfaction from his job throughout his working life. He is constantly encouraged to better himself and his qualifications and to be ambitious, so that when a more responsible post falls vacant he is ready to take over. The future foreman is made ready for his function by study in a technical institute of what is involved in the duties he will assume. And working men and women are constantly kept aware of advances in methods, invention of new materials, and probable new techniques so that they are helped to face change rather than be taken aback by it. Change is always unsettling but the disconcerting factor in it is lessened when people are gradually prepared to meet it.

This presentation of the threshold of the world of work in the GDR may seem glowing. It must be admitted that the country is not without its black sheep, drifters and rowdies, but the general ethos is such that they command no general support or admiration. The provision of sports and cultural activities is extensive, and these are in general use and provide outlets for energy. Moreover, young men and women at work rub shoulders in the Free German Youth movement with students and older pupils from the schools, so the development of an ivory-tower situation is an impossibility.

Notes to this chapter are on p 121

6

The Disadvantaged Child

SPECIAL SCHOOLS

IN the immediate post-war period, 1945–9, there were twenty-four special schools and ninety-six schools for the educationally subnormal in the then Soviet zone of Germany; today there is a total of 537 schools for the handicapped (caring for 77,901 children) and located as follows:

Berlin	22
Rostock	35
Schwerin	26
Neubrandenburg	36
Potsdam	36
Frankfurt/Oder	23
Cottbus	34
Magdeburg	43
Halle	55
Erfurt	37
Dresden	40
Leipzig	46
Karl-Marx-Stadt	57
Gera	32
Suhl	15

The overall average is 13·1 children in a class, the largest classes (14·8) being in Gera and the smallest (11·5) in Neubrandenburg. The increase in provision of special education facilities is explained by better medical diagnosis, by smaller classes and larger numbers of teachers. Considerable research has been and is being done

into root causes and remedial work, initiated by the Regulations
of 5 October 1951 on the schooling and education of children
and young people with material, physical and psychic disabili-
ties (Gesetzblatt der DDR no 122/51, p 915). By the use of
special methods in the hands of specially trained teachers, as
many children as possible are moved in the direction of normality
and the ordinary school. The aim is to equip them for work and
independent living and to integrate them into the general social
pattern. All, except the more severe cases of mental handicap,
work on the same early programme as normal children but may
take two years to do each year's work. After their second year in
school these children are divided into three groups by group
testing. Below the third group they are counted as hospital cases
and deemed ineducable.

Each school serves a specific area, providing residential accommodation for children from more distant homes or for children whose disability requires continuity of attention. The
schools cater, usually separately, for every form of handicap,
physical and mental, whether due to defect at birth or to a
subsequent accident.

THE PARTIALLY SIGHTED AND THE BLIND

There are five special schools for partially sighted children
(classed as having one-fifteenth to one twenty-fifth of normal
vision). Here they work on a full syllabus, are expected to cover
as much as possible of it, and in no circumstances less than half.
In the Pestalozzi school for partially sighted children in Halle/
Saale, for example, the children learn Russian as their first
foreign language, using oral methods and pictorial material. A
first-year class I attended was as competent and keen as any first-
year language class anywhere. For reading subjects powerful
magnifying glasses are provided, and for science, special microscopes.

For the blind there are four schools which deal with total and
almost total blindness and with very defective vision beyond the

aid of the oculist. Here again they aim at the full ten-year syllabus and the school at Königswusterhausen has the twelve-year course. To each school is attached a workshop for the blind, to give vocational training. Special apparatus, books in braille, relief maps, typewriters (these are given to the child when he leaves school) are used. A magazine published at two-monthly intervals acts as a link between researchers and teachers. From an early age the children can, but do not have to, live in residential homes which build them up to live full lives as blind people, so that they do not regard their handicap as isolating them from the rest of society.

THE DEAF AND PARTIALLY DEAF

Ten schools for the partially deaf and ten for the completely deaf, like all other special schools, cater variously for the child who is, apart from his area of disability, quite normal; for the one who is both deaf and educationally sub-normal; for children convalescing from illness which brought on deafness, for those in need of vocational training, and for the emotionally disturbed deaf who can respond to curative treatment. Children deaf from birth or who became deaf before speech habits had been established, children who have no hearing at all or so very little that they are beyond present acoustic aid (ie with a loss of more than ninety decibels) are taught by oral methods. Partially deaf children, those who cannot get speech with certainty if they are standing three metres away from the speaker (ie with a loss of more than forty decibels) use hearing aids and acoustic equipment to counteract their deafness and are also taught by oral methods. It is found, however, as in Britain and in the Soviet Union, that they communicate faster among themselves by sign language. A percentage can acquire a very small vocabulary and a limited grasp of linguistic structure, but they all learn to comprehend normal speech through lip-reading and in this way build a slender bridge between themselves and the speaking community.

E

They are expected to cover as much as possible of the syllabus of the ordinary school and to get specialist training for the wide range of jobs open to them. The more gifted can get as far as the secondary and the vocational school certificate and all are encouraged to make full use of their unimpaired faculties. This insistence on normality as a standard is a startling feature of special schools in the GDR. The state early insisted that every child, however handicapped, is part of socialist society and must be treated as such and educated to the fullest extent permitted by his disability.

THE PHYSICALLY AND MENTALLY HANDICAPPED

For the physically handicapped there are nine schools and four training centres. In addition there are special hospital schools, evenly distributed throughout the country and reserved for children who need to be under constant medical supervision: covering, for example, orthopaedic cases, amputations, certain forms of lameness, osteomyelitis, skeletal malformation, some forms of paralysis, heart and rheumatic complaints, tuberculosis of the bone and organic diseases. Schools and classes vary according to the nature of the malady and its cause. Schools for delicate children are located in particularly health-giving areas where consultants are within reach. In all cases children are encouraged to do what their handicap renders them capable of doing and essentially to live and work within its limits. The syllabus is the same as in the ordinary schools.

The newest form of special education is therapy for the under-developed child or the child whose normal development has been arrested as a result of illness. This is a field where neurologists and other consultants, psychologists and teachers work together to restore the child to a place in normal society. In the Pestalozzi school I visited in Halle, work with a first-year class was imaginatively conceived by the teacher, bringing together music, movement and original visual aids, and giving little children with

various types of arrested development some feeling of together-
ness.

The 430 Pestalozzi schools give as all-round an education as
possible to the mentally handicapped on a specially modified
syllabus, and prepare the children for a simple range of jobs.
The problems of ESN children are tackled through a study of the
nervous system in relation to physical and mental deficiencies,
particular attention being paid to their slow tempo of work and
their inability to sustain interest.

All handicapped children have practical links with factories
and workshops, even where their handicap precludes their active
participation in work. For many this contact makes sense of
school work, for in work practice adapted to their capacity they
often acquit themselves well and as a consequence the problem
of their eventual employment is eased and they more easily find
their niche in the world of work. Not only do the children become
familiar with factory work but other workers and employees
learn how to work alongside the handicapped.

TEACHING MATERIALS

For each type of handicap special textbooks have been worked
out. The first reader for the deaf appeared in 1948; German and
mathematic textbooks were published in 1951 and nature study
books followed shortly afterwards. Today there are readers,
atlases and workbooks for every school subject, geared to variously
grouped needs. Charts, cards, collections, audiovisual material,
tapes, film strips, slides and records have also been evolved for
the special schools, according to their needs, by the appropriate
department of the German Central Pedagogical Institute (now the
Academy of Pedagogical Sciences), especially since 1963. Books
for the blind come from the General Central Book Publishers
for the Blind in Leipzig. All the textbooks of the twelve-year
polytechnical secondary school, reference books, general reading
material, and even an eighteen-volume Duden's *Wörterbuch*
have been put into braille; there is a world atlas with maps in

relief, and plans, globes and astronomical charts in relief are also produced.

CONSULTATION AND TRAINING

At the Academy of Pedagogical Sciences teachers from special schools, working as a team with doctors, psychologists and teachers of normal children, are very active participants in experimentation, and their initiative and co-operation are of the utmost value in a field where the number of highly qualified educational experts is restricted. Discussions provide a means of pooling problems of a practical as well as of a theoretical nature.

The Institute for Special School Work at the Humboldt University in Berlin has two-year courses for teachers with normal training who wish to become teachers of the handicapped. Teachers of the educationally subnormal are trained in the University of Halle.

CARE OF THE SLIGHTLY HANDICAPPED

Even where a handicap appears slight it is recognised as a grave disadvantage in schoolwork and it may be symptomatic of illness requiring medical attention. A child with a slight handicap may continue to work in an ordinary school but get appropriate help in out-of-school hours, for overcoming or coming to terms with the handicap. For instance, children with slight speech defects attend ordinary schools and have speech therapy in out-of-school time. A peripatetic speech-trainer takes the worst cases herself, working under a doctor's direction, and advises the school about the help to be given to less severe cases. Where severe speech defects, stammering among them, are not due to ir-remediable causes like damage to hearing or brain or to permanent mental handicap, children may attend a special kindergarten in Rostock and then from six years on go to whichever school, special or ordinary, best fits their needs and aptitudes. Those who have some chance of a permanent cure are advised to attend boarding schools and have the benefit of individualised specialist care at the local hospital. Among resources used are sleep therapy,[1] psychotherapy and medical aid. Such schools take cases of cleft-palate and work with remedial centres whose aim is to make full use of what speech a child has.

As in other developed countries, there is increasing emphasis on early diagnosis in order to substitute, where possible, preventive for remedial work.

CHILDREN'S HOMES

Children's homes are of two kinds: those for children from unsatisfactory homes or in need of care and protection, unwanted children and orphans; and special homes for young offenders.

The youth welfare organisation and welfare workers, found in every town, do not take the step of placing a child in a home until all else has failed. Orphans and children in need of care are then sometimes put in foster homes; others are looked after in children's homes either until their own home achieves a greater degree of adequacy or throughout the years of compulsory schooling. Here the children have tutors, like housemothers, whose work it is to provide care and love and to foster group relations to compensate in some measure for the children's own poor homes. The homes at kindergarten level are full of good toys, play materials and personal possessions. Some of the best equipment I have ever seen anywhere was at the Morgenrot home in Bernberg. At Stollberg in the Harz, one of the many homes set in lovely country, the director and his family live close to the boys and girls, and it is obvious that this arrangement, together with the good food, healthful activity and attendance at the local school, has a stabilising effect.

There are homes for ESN children; homes for young people of sixteen to eighteen who are taught a trade; homes and boarding schools for problem children, and for children with nerve disorders. All these are ordinary homes from which the children go out to school. But there are also the special homes for young offenders, children out of hand and at variance with the law, and in these schooling is provided on the premises. But before a child is sent to one of these an effort is made to discover a reason for the delinquency, to see if perhaps a broken home can be pieced together and conditions of life for the child be bettered. When this fails, youth welfare assumes full responsibility and refers the matter to a committee which makes a decision about transference to a home for a determined period if the child is under fourteen. Should the need be prolonged beyond the specified period, a home is not thought of as a permanent solution. Adoption is preferred, the attitude being that parents who have failed to exercise parental responsibility, despite the aid of school committee and workmates, lose the right to parenthood—a line only taken as a last resort. But if the child returns to his own home liaison work is done by the special home where he has been cared for.

If the delinquent is in the fourteen to twenty age group, he lives in a hostel for nine to eighteen months and goes out to work from there, getting vocational education that will lead to a trade qualification.

In 1967–8 there were about 26,000 children and young folk in homes of both kinds. The numbers in each establishment vary from thirty to eighty, one or two tutors, mainly women, looking after every fifteen children. Tutors in the ordinary children's homes are concerned with secondary training and specialise in crafts, horticulture, music or art: they are assisted by non-specialists with an interest in this type of work. Tutors who work in special homes take training as for teachers of educationally subnormal children. There is an Institute for Youth Welfare Workers at Ludwigsfelde, whose students make a special study of maladjustment and the appropriate therapy.

In all homes Pioneer and Free Youth groups are formed, to help provide a normal, happy and useful life.

Notes to this chapter are on p 121

7
Youth Clubs and Movements

CENTRAL PIONEER HOUSE

EVERYONE who has visited Moscow remembers the Pioneer Palace, its spacious, artistic layout, its multifarious activities and the first-class facilities it offers the city's young people. It would be difficult for any country to parallel that, nor can the Central Pioneer House in Berlin do so. But the Berlin house itself is spacious: the building was formerly a school and before it was made over to Berlin children in 1949 it was reconditioned and adapted to its new use by Soviet architects and workmen. The building has been beautified with paintings, woodcuts, ceramics, pottery, carving and the decorative use of plants; club members feel a personal responsibility for keeping it scrupulously clean and tidy. The state makes a direct grant of 1·7M million a year for the upkeep and running of the house.

Pioneer groups from all areas of the city delegate children of nine and over to take part in the various activities, but any child with an interest in any one hobby can come on his own. Within its spacious walls are all the elements of a gigantic youth club catering for all age groups and every sort of home background. It is a place where children can have a very full life of their own, finding outlets for physical energy and creativeness under the general guidance of a body of forty-four pioneer leaders who are trained teachers. There are also many auxiliary helpers and some eighty musicians, actors and professional people whose help is available; public figures, parents and older members of the Free

German Youth Movement (the group for young people from fifteen to twenty-five) co-operate, too. Direction is wise but not obtrusive or restrictive; the atmosphere is friendly and informal and the children uninhibited. The house is freely open to visitors from abroad and is paralleled by some 116 other Pioneer Houses in the Republic.

AIMS AND ACTIVITIES

The avowed aims of all these Pioneer Houses are:

a. to further inclinations, gifts and talents;

b. to back up the work done in schools by organising exhibitions and showing films connected with the school syllabus;

c. to reinforce the work of the Pioneer organisations in the schools by offering facilities that would not be accessible to smaller groups;

d. to bring a wide variety of experiences to the children in a less formal atmosphere than that of the classroom.

There are in all 130 activities in the Berlin house grouped into six broad departments.

Cultural subjects   This is the largest department and includes a children's symphony orchestra with ninety-six players, in whose training the Pro-Rector of the German Institute for Music, Hans Eislen, has taken an active part. The members travel to give concerts and to study in other countries. There is also a choir with 180 voices, a folk music (instrumental) group of 65 and dance groups involving 96 members. There are a children's theatre, a puppet theatre and a shadow theatre with their opportunities for learning stagecraft and script-writing, an art club for painting, drawing and pottery, societies for young historians, young librarians, young writers (who produce a well illustrated and imaginative journal), and circles for art and music appreciation.

Technical groups   These, with laboratories, tools and machines where appropriate, are run in co-operation with firms, trade unions, interested workmen, tradesmen, scientists and engineers. Up and down the country there are young technician stations where young people can try out experiments in the technical field. In the Pioneer House itself one group is concerned with electro-technics and radio construction, another with chemistry and another with boat-building. There is a motor mechanics club with a driving school, and a cosmonauts club where children learn something about cosmonaut training, test their own reactions in simulated space flight conditions, hear tapes, see films, make models, study maps and catch up on astronomy.

Young naturalists The Berlin Pioneer House runs two greenhouses, a terrarium and a biology station for animal rearing. It also has stations for the study of rare plants and for experimenting with various types of cultivation.

Sport Opportunities are provided for all forms of athletics and all kinds of team games—including ice hockey and skating.

Travel and international friendship Young tourist stations encourage the desire to travel, arrange for members to see their own and other accessible countries, receive visitors from other countries (mainly, though not exclusively, from Warsaw Pact countries). The international friendship circle has a link with that of the Pioneer Palace in Moscow.

Library The house has a free library of about 10,000 volumes; borrowers can take out three books for a loan period of three weeks. It is a free-access library and attractively laid out.

THE VALUE OF PIONEER HOUSES

There is no compulsion on any child to frequent the house or on the parents to encourage him to do so. But it represents a purposeful, absorbing use of free time along so very many lines, with materials and tools in profusion and a deep and wide fund of informed advice which no parent could provide, that membership is highly regarded by children and parents alike. A visitor to the GDR does not see children and youths drifting aimlessly round and loafing about in the towns. This is partly because of the general attitude to life and work, but also because young people have 'somewhere to go and something to do'.

Pioneer leaders from the schools can also pursue their interests at the Pioneer House and even do a two-year re-training course in Pioneer work, on a bi-monthly seminar/lecture basis, learning new skills that they would like to be competent to use. They help with the children and so acquire experience under guidance.

PIONEER GROUPS IN SCHOOLS

Children of six to nine in classes 1–3 are Young Pioneers and correspond in some ways to the Young Octobrists of the Soviet Union. They describe the blue scarf they wear as part of the blue flag of the Free German Youth (to which organisation they will belong), and as such it is greatly respected. They have a newspaper of their own, entitled *ABC*. Each group is run by a trained Pioneer leader who is often a tutor in the school.

In classes 4–8, ages nine to fourteen, the children are grouped as Thälmann Pioneers. They promise to 'learn, work and fight as Ernst Thälmann teaches'.[1] They pay an infinitesimal entrance fee of 10 pfennig and have a right to all the club and sports facilities provided in the Pioneer section of the school and the Pioneer House, and a place in the Pioneer holiday camps. The laws they undertake to observe are faintly reminiscent of the rules for Soviet schoolchildren, formulated in 1943, and listed by Nigel Grant in his *Soviet Education*.[2]

The badge of the Pioneers bears the initials JP (*Junge Pioniere*) on a blue ground with three leaping yellow flames and the motto 'Be ready'. Their flag is their badge on a blue ground with the motto 'For peace and socialism ever ready'. This formula is used in many classrooms: when the teacher is ready to begin the lesson she asks the standing children or the monitor in charge 'Ist Klasse 4 bereit?' (Is class 4 ready?), and receives the reply 'Immer bereit' (Ever ready) pronounced with the palm of the hand on and at right angles to the head.

On important occasions the girls wear a white blouse and dark skirt, the boys a white shirt and dark shorts, both displaying the blue scarf. On ordinary school days they wear whatever they like for school, with or without the scarf.

Pioneers and FDJs in schools act for a day at a time and once a fortnight in a capacity similar to that of prefects in an English school. When on duty they are recognisable by their red arm bands (like orderly officers!), but there is a lot of debate about the desirable age for the exercise of this authority.

FREE GERMAN YOUTH MOVEMENT

The FDJ (*Freie Deutsche Jugend*—Free German Youth Movement) is for the age group fifteen to twenty-five and corresponds to the Soviet Union's Young Komsomols. Their uniform is a blue shirt or blouse worn with a dark skirt or trousers. Their badge is a blue shield with a rising sun and the letters FDJ, and this symbol is also on their blue flag. This group is for the older pupils at school, students at all levels, young soldiers and youth out at work, and performs the function of merging young people, however divergent their interests, into an organisation of contemporaries. At national level the organisation has a Parliament of its own which meets once every four years and is addressed by the head of state; it also has a Central Council that meets once every four months. At local level, in region, district, city, or rural area, conferences are held once in three months.

Membership of the organisation presupposes a high sense of social awareness, a high standard of ethics and morality, and good standards of discipline and responsibility. It is seen as a patriotic duty to belong to the FDJ and as a personal and social duty to work through and for it. Members avow a strong determination to see that there will never be another-war started by Germans and fought on German soil, and Lenin's advice to 'learn, learn and again learn', whether at school or at work, is taken seriously. With self-discipline is coupled a sense of social responsibility for the beauty and pleasantness of the environment, in school, home and city. The great emphasis is on self-help.

The leisure pursuits enjoined are reading, music (vocal and

instrumental), visits to museums and art galleries, theatre and cinema going, participation in games, sports, hikes, trips, travel and pre-military training.

There is no condoning of selfishness and immorality; vandalism is judged anti-social and a violation of the respect due to the work of another; in relations with young and old, friends and all others, there is an awareness of people, of their rights and desires and claims, and a great respect for all work and for those who do it. This classlessness is a very notable feature of the society in which they live, where the factory manager and the apprentice, the taxi driver and his passenger, sit at the same table with no self-consciousness on either side. Mutual respect and courtesy, especially to older people, are held in high regard.

Failure to observe the rules of the FDJ, if persistent, can lead to the one real sanction, which is ejection. Ejection means rejection, for the testimony of the FDJ group is essential to career success.

Young people in the GDR count, and have the right to be outspoken in criticism, to voice opinions. They are taken seriously, given responsibility, made to feel how much they matter. 'Everybody is somebody' and everyone has the possibility of living a full life.

But admittedly not everyone is burning with conviction: it requires such a high level of constant effort and motions alone do not change situations. There is also the question whether convictions can be transmitted by reiteration. On psychological grounds it is conceivable that in some cases the reverse result of that envisaged might be brought about. Many people have relations in West Germany, and though censorship of books is strict, ideas do float and filter in. They float and filter out too: in a speech to the delegates of the Eighth Parliament of the FDJ (12 May 1967, quoted in *Sozialistisches Bildungsrecht*) Herr Ulbricht stressed that youth in the GDR feels close to the youth in the FDR.[3]

Notes to this chapter are on p 121

8

Parents

FIRST CONTACT WITH SCHOOL

PARENTS first come into formal contact with the school to which their child goes when his sixth birthday is past. The child, in his last year of nursery school, has spent half a day a week in a reception class to accustom himself to the more formal world of school. On the Sunday before term begins he comes to school with both his parents and is received in the school hall with music, a talk by the headteacher and a concert given by slightly older children. After meeting his new teacher, he is taken by an older child to his classroom, where he finds a posy on his desk (one of thirty identical posies); a register is called, his schoolbooks, bag, lunch satchel, writing materials are checked and then he is taken off to a party in the school dining-room. As far as the child is concerned, the whole idea is to emphasise that the first day of school is a great day in his life; parents or grandparents give him a huge fancy cornet (*Tüte*) filled with sweets and toys; photos are taken; it is a day of rejoicing. As he enjoys the feasting, his parents sit in his classroom and learn from the staff what the school wants to do for their child and what part they must play in collaborating with it. For it has long been recognised that if home and school pull in opposite directions the principal sufferer is the child.

Both parents are asked to return the following Wednesday evening, ready to take notes and be told how their child is settling in. On that day they will also elect five to seven of their

77

number to form a parents' committee (*das Klassenelternaktiv*) for that class. This committee holds office for two years and delegates one of its number to the Parents' Council for the whole school. Both parents are expected to come to general parents' meetings and to participate in things that affect the class's well-being. They must be willing to co-operate with the teacher and the class-tutor in anything that affects the progress of the children, and be ready to help other parents who may have difficulties of one sort or another. The schools are normally neighbourhood schools and parents already know each other to some extent and may even be workmates together. Normally teachers do not assume office on the parents' committees and councils of the school their child attends.

PARENTS AS EDUCATORS

It is never lost sight of that the natural environment for the child is its home and that its first educators are the parents: their care of their children is a responsibility they have to the community and one they are encouraged to face. Consequently great importance is attached to the home, the first training ground, and much is done to help parents with the skilled business of bringing up children. This sense of solidarity with others, the knowledge that advice and help are at hand for any who need them, and the involvement of fathers as well as mothers in child-rearing and guidance makes for responsible parenthood. Marriage is seen as an equal partnership and the cosseted role of the pre-war German husband and father is a thing of the past. Normally both parents work, are often politically or socially active, and within the home they share all the duties that make a home a real one.

As members of society all children, furthermore, are the care of all grown-ups, and to see any child doing something anti-social and not to intervene is regarded as a dereliction of duty to society (*Family Law of the GDR*, State Publishing House, Berlin 1966, 11 par 3).

In a printed letter sent out to all parents at the beginning of the school year, not only are indications given of what school-work and general training the child will get, but also of what parents can do actively to help their own child and to make his schooling a joyous experience. Parents are asked not to teach their children formally but to stimulate their curiosity and their powers of self-expression, verbally and in drawing. The psychological needs of young children in relation to physical development are set out in simple language and explained as to co-partners with the teacher in the educational process. Later, the responsibility of sex education is placed squarely on the shoulders of parents. Although a doctor's advice can be made available and although some teachers are prepared to help, the whole question of sexual relations within the context of society is dealt with by the parents.

The child has to come to school ready to be self-dependent, with road-sense, a sense of obedience that owes nothing to threats of corporal punishment, and a feeling for order on which the school can build. In the home, too, the child gets its first notions of respect for work and for the man who does it, and learns to behave so that he himself does not spoil that work.

PARENT-TEACHER RELATIONSHIPS

Parents have access to the class-tutors and the teachers in school, and may attend their children's lessons at any time. Each class has a tutor (form-teacher, educator) who works closely with staff, children and parents. She arranges meetings for the parents of her class and as she is trained for the work she can guide discussions among parents, many of whom have much to learn but also much to contribute. But the aim is to involve the parents as a group, while not avoiding the question of parents everywhere: 'How is he doing?'.

As a form of social work all teachers are required to make one visit a year to the home of each pupil, always by pre-arrangement. This is not primarily a social call but an educational exercise, and if a friendly atmosphere is created, frank interchange of views is possible. Problems over TV viewing, insufficient sleep, job-counselling and so on can rise to the surface in an informal atmosphere. Another form of parent-teacher contact is by written communications, which may be of a congratulatory or a hortatory nature.

The parent is important, but there is never any question of his taking over. The teacher remains the master of his own classroom as the headmaster is the master of the school.

THE PARENTS' COUNCIL

Social work can be done by parents for the school either through the Parents' Council or independently, as, for instance, laying out school grounds, taking part in rambles, museum visits, sports activities, and, where feasible, in giving help for the many competitions which are such a feature of life in the Republic. They are quite often involved in career discussions, sometimes in travel talks and, in rural areas, in practical questions on farming, cultivation and farm machinery.

The Parents' Council helps and advises the headmaster or mistress on the general welfare and policy of the school in so far as the interests of the parents are concerned. If it gets at variance with the head, appeal can be made to the local education officer. But generally it upholds the authority of the head and for this reason some teachers have seen the Parents' Council as a menace, 'a lengthening of the arm of the headteacher'.

In the closely knit community of school and neighbourhood there is little or no place for inter-generation conflict, though adolescents grow to independence as they do the world over. To some people, especially those outside the GDR, the whole social and educational system may appear inflexible; but it does produce a clean, active and purposeful society—the antithesis of the permissive society—and it brings so many agencies into play on behalf of young people, places so many opportunities at their disposal and encourages them to work hard, play hard and live their lives fully but not for themselves alone.

9
Teachers and their Training

STATUS AND ATTITUDE OF TEACHERS

IN official declarations it is repeatedly stressed that teachers deserve the respect, backing and affection not only of those they teach but of the whole nation because of the important work they do. They certainly play a key role in the socialist fabric, and by their knowledge and skill it is theirs to teach and train up successive generations. With the co-operation of state and local agencies, and with research and scientific bodies to help, they are able to concentrate their whole effort on teaching. The close linkage between home, school and the sponsoring factory or business concern is also a support to the teacher. Moreover, youth club work and children's out-of-school interests not only do not militate against the aims of the school, but co-operate actively in their achievement.

Yet the teacher does not see the pupil merely as someone to be taught. He is expected to be concerned with the welfare of the child both in and out of school; this is part of his duty to working-class people and to their ideals and welfare. Any teacher who found himself at variance with this conception of his duty would have no place in the school. In any case every teacher has, himself, a worker's qualification.

Long before UNESCO was developing the theme of permanent education the teacher in the GDR was being expected to add to his qualifications, to keep himself in a state of constant renewal, to be a life-long learner, stretched to the limit of his possibilities. He is expected to work hard and does so. As in all countries, the teaching ability of the individual varies and so, in direct ratio, does the attitude of the children to his subject. When one teacher said 'German children find Russian difficult', it was patent that her dull methods were at fault, whereas a colleague in another school was able to rouse and sustain enthusiasm for the language by skilled and lively teaching.

TEACHER TRAINING—NURSERY SCHOOL

There is a central policy for teacher training and this is adapted at various levels in the different types of training colleges. The attitude is adopted that no one who wants to teach must be rejected and that the right training will produce the right teacher. Certainly the course at all levels and in all institutions is a thorough and searching one.

Nursery school superintendents are prepared in the thirteen pedagogical schools. The entrance requirement is the leaving certificate of the ten-year polytechnical school or practical experience with young children. The course of full-time study for the first of these groups lasts two years; for those who go in as nursery-school auxiliaries, the course is by correspondence and lasts three years. The students train for all three age groups in the nursery school. They study German language and literature, numbers, nature, speech training, art, music (they must be able to play an instrument) and hygiene. They must also study Marxism-Leninism, as the philosophy of the society in which they and the children live, and they learn enough educational psychology to help them handle young children wisely and to appreciate the value of play.

They do a four-week supervised practice in a nursery school and at the end of the course have a state oral and practical examination; the only written exercise is a twenty-page thesis on a theme allied with their work. They then work under supervision for two years.

TEACHER TRAINING—GENERAL

Teacher training for compulsory schooling and beyond is at present taken at three levels and in different establishments. There is still admittedly a certain amount of distinction between the levels of teaching. By 1975 it is proposed to narrow the gap and to unify existing establishments, teachers' institutes and pedagogical institutes, just as the three great teachers' colleges of Potsdam, Erfurt and Dresden have been made comprehensive and university departments virtually abolished. Teaching staffs in training establishments are already being prepared for this unification, as they are made ready well in advance whenever there are to be major changes in the curriculum of the schools. It is noteworthy that no teacher need spend all his career at the level for which he has been trained if he is willing to put in the very considerable amount of work entailed in taking a correspondence course, or a full-time course for the next higher level.

THE TEACHER-TRAINING INSTITUTE

To enter a teacher-training institute a student must have secured the leaving certificate of the ten-year school or reached an equivalent standard in a vocational school, or have, as a working man, done a correspondence course to reach the same level. He then has to spend four years at the college, engaged part of the time on widening and deepening his own education and part of the time on subjects specifically geared to teaching classes 1–3 in the polytechnical secondary school.

The study of German language and literature, new mathematics (which many find very hard), and one elective subject (sport, music, handwork or art) is compulsory for all students. But syllabuses in all four are so wide that they have to work hard to cover the ground. In addition they study the methodology of their subjects, the educational psychology of children between the ages of six and nine, and Marxism-Leninism.

The institute year is divided into two parts (semesters) and in the first part of the second year, the student spends three weeks in introductory practice, which enables him to see the top class in the nursery school and to observe work in the first three classes of the polytechnical school. During the holidays between years two and three, he has to spend some time in a Pioneer holiday camp, organising activities for the whole age group. At the end of the third year he does his practice of four weeks (in the sixth semester) observing each year but teaching mostly in classes 2 and 3.

The preparation for both practices, but especially for the first, is very rigorous. From his teacher-tutor as well as from the institute supervisor, he learns how to prepare and evaluate lessons and acquires professional standards. He does not work in isolation but with the little group of fellow-students practising in the same school, one of them being elected as leader—often one already accustomed to organising in the Free German Youth Movement. Such a group going into a class to observe forms a team, and each looks at a different aspect of the lesson given by the teacher-tutor, the member of the school staff deputed by the local education authority, in consultation with the headteacher, to be their adviser. They decide among themselves which is to be responsible for which aspect. They are free to question the teacher-tutor (as they are free to discuss with their own lecturers the value of their theoretical instruction) and to bring up any discrepancies they have found between theory and practice. The students make a study of the class they visit, consider the books they use, collect specimens of work, account in detail for class participation or non-participation, count out the proportion of time monopolised by the teacher, the degree and type of class involvement, entering their findings on work sheets provided by the college. They make a study of the official syllabus and see how the lessons observed fit into it, so that when the day comes for them to try their own hand at teaching their contributions become part of the scheme and no time is wasted. (How many students giving lessons at secondary level in England ever see work schemes into which their lessons are to fit?) In addition each student is directed to take a personal interest in two children who may be falling behind and to give them an hour of his time in the afternoons to help them to catch up.

This first practice is minutely mapped out. The reporting that the student is required to do is really a training, a breaking in to the business of teaching. This is not a rather bored sitting in on lessons, with only a vague notion of how to observe and what to look for, but an exercise in analysis and evaluation. It might be thought that such detailed instructions cut out all students to one pattern. This is far from being the case, as the diversity in classrooms testifies, but the system proceeds on the theory that teaching is a science and that scientific norms have to be applied. Learning to teach is like learning a trade: until the craft is mastered, experiment is a rash operation.

In the second practice less time is spent in observation and more in teaching with the teacher-tutor and fellow-students present, but only two lessons are attended by the institute supervisor, acting in an advisory capacity. The practical examination and the oral are conducted by an examination commission on which the supervisor, the headmaster of the school, the local education officer and a member of the Free German Youth organisation sit; and the thesis required is a carefully prepared and presented piece of work, as are the detailed notes for the examination lesson.

Ultimately the headmasters or headmistresses (no distinction is made in a country where equal pay for equal work, whatever the work, is the rule) of the practising schools are responsible for the progress of the student.[1]

THE PEDAGOGICAL INSTITUTE—ENTRY

The choice of institute   Teachers for the top classes (4–10) have to be subject specialists and train in one of the pedagogical institutes in Güstrow, Halle, Köthen, Leipzig, Magdeburg and Zwickau, which offer allied subjects among the standard combinations: German/history; Russian/English; mathematics/physics; mathematics/chemistry; chemistry/biology; polytechnics. The areas of particular excellence in any one institute are related to the distinction of its director in a particular field of work. Students who wish to teach in the extended secondary school may attend one of the larger pedagogical institutes, namely Potsdam or Erfurt, or pursue their studies at a university.

Students apply to the institute of their choice: if it happens to be in their home town they are already known to the staff of the institute through the latter's contact with the schools. To be accepted they must have successfully completed the twelve-year extended secondary school course, and produce the evidence of their leaving certificate. In addition, all prospective students are required to visit, on an open day, the institute they are about to enter to meet the staff and be made fully aware of the details of the course. There is no dearth of places.

Pre-course work   Before actually starting the course the student attends a six-week summer camp which provides an initiation into methods of working and study, and, for men, a little pre-military training. The camp also offers a full-time one-year course for workers coming forward to be teachers. This year gives them the basics of subject study so that they can join with confidence the next first-year classes of the institute. The only difference in courses thereafter is that they have to study German more intensively and do no Russian, whereas students coming straight from school continue with Russian.

ORGANISATION OF THE PEDAGOGICAL INSTITUTE COURSE

General subjects   The course is a four-year one and includes classes in Marxism-Leninism, the scientific bases of education, didactics, the history of education, some incidental comparative education, psychology and one major and one minor subject, which are the special subjects which the student intends to teach. The minor subject is state-examined in year three, and the major subject in the last year, as is also the student's grasp of Marxism-Leninism. The courses in Marxism-Leninism are concerned with the politico-economic life of the country, the role of social philosophy in job-doing, the history of the German workers' movement, dialectical and historical materialism and the political economy of capitalism and socialism.

The requirement of Russian for all, except for ex-workers, demands the ability to read round their subjects in the language, to translate it and know how to use it in writing and speaking on their subjects.

First-year physical education is for the student's own health, and includes gymnastics, games and swimming; in the second year he may concentrate on the activity he prefers—it may be athletics, gymnastics or a game—so that he will have a positive contribution to make later on to the life of a school. Any student excused from physical activity on medical grounds learns to judge and referee.

All students are given instruction in the legal aspects of the profession they have chosen.

The study of education   The study of education, in so far as the scientific bases are concerned, is closely allied with Marxist thinking. Didactics deal with the general principles running through all teaching and to them is added the methodology of the separate specialist teaching subjects; the history of education is widely conceived and includes the study of great educational thinkers in Germany and other countries. Psychology lectures deal currently with personality development within the social framework: the development of individual gifts within and for society, not for self-gratification.

Teaching subjects   It is patently impossible to deal with all of these even in a most general way, but the biology syllabus, the speciality of Halle Pedagogical Institute, may be cited as an example. It covers plant, animal and human physiology, the origin of species, genetics, ecology and its relations with geography. It is not only factual but is applied to social living, the needs of agriculture and forestry, medicine, pharmacy and includes micro- and molecular studies. Lectures, practicals and fieldwork all draw on the student's knowledge of chemistry, mathematics and physics.

Polytechnics are regarded as the single most important area of socialist education. To specialise in them requires a sound basic knowledge of mathematics and science subjects and these are intensively pursued in the institute. The future polytechnic teacher must acquire comprehensive technical knowledge so that he can eventually prepare his pupils in classes 4–10 for the world of work and all that that implies. He will have his own special interest, for example a branch of engineering, but he must know about allied trades and be able to teach manual work in classes 4–6, all-round technical subjects including technical drawing in classes 7–10 and to give the theoretical background of the productive work done by pupils in classes 7 and 8. And he must be in contact with a factory throughout his course. Indeed, all the science staff are expected to take part in factory discussions, for each department is linked with a factory, a business concern or a farm to the increased effectiveness of which its own research work might make a contribution and from which it can receive various kinds of help.

Scientific research   The Academy of Pedagogical Sciences assigns to each pedagogical institute an area of research. In Halle, where the course is science orientated, the allotted specialisation is parasitology, and staff and students engage together on the research project. From the beginning of the third year when they begin to concentrate more heavily on their academic subject, they are initiated into research methods so that each department has a special research profile, with staff/student teams and all students doing two hours practical laboratory work a day.

School practice   During the course, school practice is done in three parts. At the end of year one, practice in a summer Pioneer camp is obligatory after one week's preparation, and all students have to do Pioneer/Free German Youth work as a social

duty and as an element in their training. In year two there is a
regular amount of observation of good teaching minutely
analysed and discussed with the teacher giving the lesson in the
demonstration school and with a team of institute lecturers who
have also seen the lesson. The first half of year four is devoted
to school practice under the supervision of teacher-tutors and
special staff from the institute. At this level teacher-tutors are
paid 100M a semester per student per subject.

Examinations   Method, education, psychology and school
health are examined in year four by oral tests; sample lessons,
with rigorously presented notes, are given before an examination
commission; a thirty to thirty-five-page thesis, or a piece of
practical work produced and written up, certified by the student
as his own work or that of his team, concludes the examinations.

STUDENTS AND STAFF

Lecturers are expected to co-operate with each other, to attend
each other's lectures and to interest themselves in the welfare of
the students whom they get to know very well both in and out
of class.

Students are encouraged, in all of their classes, to give free
expression to their views in any area, be it political, social or
educational. They are quite free to discuss with the lecturers
concerned how far the way the work is conceived and the
emphasis placed on it meet their aspirations and requirements.

Administration   A council in each department in the institute forwards recommendations to the institute council, on which
there is 50 per cent student representation and which meets
three times a year. Its views are sent to the rector. There is in the
institute, too, a research council which also exercises a controlling
function.

The institutes vary in size and may have between 1,000 and
2,000 full-time students,[2] about half or a third of them living in
hostels, mostly rooming in twos, paying 70M for full board and

8M a month for lodgings. They have student unions, a bar and spacious campuses.

Student grants   The highest grant of 190M a month goes to ex-members of the armed forces, to men with experience of production or to those whose parents were workers or party members prior to 1945, known anti-nazis or presently in the service of the state, or earn a joint salary of 1,000M.

A grant of 140M goes to those with parents in administration or in private business with an income of 400M a month or less. Into the same category come the children of teachers and working men. Others get 80M a month, with, where appropriate, a child allowance of 30M, or of 70M, where help has to be hired. If the student is married there is a 10 per cent increase if the wife is working and earning over 250M a month; a 20 per cent increase if she earns less than 250M a month. There are extra grants for very good work, free health service and insurance against accidents.

Teaching staff   Normally those who are appointed to teach in a pedagogical institute have five years' experience of special subject teaching at school level. Very good past students may be taken on when they have had two to three years' experience: these will have been encouraged to aim at the institute. They are first engaged as assistants to take classes and to prepare a doctoral thesis in education, about the equivalent of an English PhD, which they are required to defend orally before the examiners, as well as submitting to an oral examination in basic philosophy. If this work is thought to be good enough, they are then invited (or may themselves suggest it) to prepare for the *Habilitazion* which requires a piece of serious original research and corresponds to an English doctorate in science or letters. From the ranks of those with this research qualification or with the doctorate in education, lecturers and professors are chosen, but a post in a pedagogical institute does not automatically follow. A percentage of people with very high qualifications are ploughed back into the schools, as a matter of policy.

TRAINING FOR EXTENDED SECONDARY SCHOOL TEACHING

Teachers for the extended secondary school train in one of the universities, or in Potsdam or Erfurt which are multidisciplinary institutes of very high standing. They may also be trained in the institutes of Güstrow, Halle, Leipzig, Dresden, or Karl-Marx-Stadt; those specialising in physical education train at the PE institute at Leipzig; those specialising in music at the music institute in Weimar.

The entrance qualification is the successful completion of the *Abitur* course and a period of social service. Those who intend to become specialists in polytechnical education can go to the polytechnical institutes of the universities of Berlin, Dresden or Halle. In the latter university there has been much research into the whole subject of integrated polytechnical teaching and its complex methodology for both urban and rural occupations. This has been the work of Professor H. Wolfgramm and his very highly specialised team of scientists, who have also recently done some good advance planning on the work of the institute up to the year 2000, as well as some valuable analysis on weaknesses in the schoolteaching their students have received and how these might be overcome.

THE WORK AND TRAINING OF HEADMASTERS, HEADMISTRESSES AND ADMINISTRATORS

A special feature of East German education (and one not yet developed in the Soviet Union) is the training of administrators, including headmasters and future occupiers of such posts. Teachers who wish to earn this type of promotion or who are invited to prepare for it are recommended by their local education authority for the course at Potsdam Pedagogical Institute. It consists of one year's full-time study and six months' part-time study including the preparation of a thesis. A diploma in educational administration is awarded at the end of the course.

The subjects covered are Marxism-Leninism, education, psychology, educational planning, handling of man-power resources, and current problems and policies in the running of a school. Students discuss problems both in the context of the school and in the wider context of society; they discuss the function of the school as a place for the development of social democracy. They become familiar with the principles of time-table construction, data processing and educational machines of various kinds. They also study the problems of personal relationships with pupils, colleagues, parents, and the question of leadership, control, criticism and appreciation.

Incorporated with the theory, the seminars and the discussion groups, is a fortnight's practice in a situation analogous to the one for which they are preparing. The weekly load is twenty hours and the work is arranged in monthly assignments. In 1970–1 there were twenty-five heads or future heads on the course.

This preparation is deemed a valuable training for one who has great responsibilities to the Ministry of Education and to the society which confides children to his care. The headteacher is fully responsible for his staff. He has to help each individual teacher plan his year's work in conformity with the central syllabuses, to suggest realistic norms, restructuring where the proposed course seems to demand it. He is expected to build up the weaker teacher by diagnosing and advising on the weakness, even by giving him a reduced teaching load and sending him to observe a good teacher at work in some other school. He has also to know which members of his staff ought to be encouraged to take further qualifications. He has to maintain the necessary close links with the factory or business concern that sponsors his school and to be available to parents generally, but particularly to parents with problems. In addition he is expected to put in some teaching in his specialist area (five or six periods a week).

TUTORS AND PIONEER LEADERS

There are two further groups of trainees. These are the tutors

(*Erzieher*) who act as form teachers or work in whole-day schools helping with homework and other activities and who make links with home and youth movement. Their training varies with the type and level of work they want to do and many prepare themselves by correspondence courses, but roughly speaking they get the formation for teachers for classes 1–3.

The other main group is that of the Pioneer leaders who mostly train in the Central School of the Pioneer organisation at Droyssig, again as for classes 1–3, but taking special Pioneer training.

RE-TRAINING AND REFRESHER COURSES

In view of rapid change in every aspect of life and learning, the need for re-training has long been recognised and is now enforced. Teachers in the Republic have always been encouraged to bring themselves up to date or to upgrade their qualifications. Today the law requires every teacher to re-train in subjects and their methodology and in Marxism-Leninism for four weeks in the year every four years (a) on full-time leave from school; (b) by correspondence, with part-time attendance in the holidays; (c) by holiday courses. In October the courses deal with the political/ideological area; in February with the educational/psychological subjects; in July with subject knowledge and new ideas on its methodology: in all twenty-three days or four weeks. In each year 25 per cent of all teachers re-train in their own holidays.[3] It will be evident that such courses have to be intensive and to utilise to the full the available time. They take place in the chief towns, at the Teachers' Centre for Berlin teachers, or at the Institute for Inservice Training at Ludwigsfelde and Potsdam. The re-training is in the first place a fortifying of socialist convictions through a renewed and deepened study of the underlying philosophy; and in the second it is a fresh insight into the subject matter of the teacher's specialisation, geared to the level at which he teaches it, though there is also the opportunity to examine a subject in which he has as yet no qualifications. In this way teachers are kept informed of new research of a scholarly and practical nature affecting them and their work.

SALARY SCALES

There are no salary differences between men and women. Teachers retire at the age of sixty-five (men) or of sixty (women) but if the teacher elects to stay on after retirement age he may draw, concurrently, his pension (60 per cent of his salary in the last year of teaching) and his salary. There are marriage allowances, children's allowances after the second child and a whole range of allowances for additional responsibility. Rises were forecast at the last Pedagogical Congress but sample available figures for Berlin (a little higher than in other towns) are as follows:

1. Workmen who become practical subject teachers in classes 3–8: 495M a month rising by (ten) two-yearly increments to 590M.

2. Teachers in classes 1–3: 545M a month rising by (five) two-yearly increments to 815M.

3. Teachers in classes 4–10: 625M a month rising to a maximum of 870M.

A teacher can rise into another group if he is recommended as a good teacher, even without further qualifications.

4. Teachers in classes 9–12 (EOS): 685M a month rising to a maximum of 945M.

5. Teachers in technical schools preparing for the diploma: 710M a month rising to a maximum of 990M.

Local directors of education and local advisers come into this range and must have qualifications for teaching in class 12.

6. Training institute lecturers with full qualifications: 750M a month rising to a maximum of 1,020M.

7. Headmaster of a small factory vocational school: 860M a month rising to a maximum of 1,050M.

8. Headmaster of a large factory vocational school: 885M a month rising to a maximum of 1,075M.

Special allowances are available as follows:

1. Anyone teaching three age ranges together (a relic of the past and operative in very few cases): additional 40M a month.

2. Peripatetic teacher: additional 40M a month.

3. Teachers in special schools: additional 60M a month.

4. Teachers acting as Pioneer House leaders: additional 100M a month.

5. Teachers acting as out-of-school instructors (in the afternoon at a whole-day school): additional 150M a month.

6. Technical School Inspector: additional 160M a month.

7. Area Inspector: additional 120M a month.

8. Sport instruction in a school with 200 pupils: additional 60M a month.

9. Head of an institute with 300 or more students: additional 260M a month.

10. Head of a ten-year school: additional 160M a month.

11. Head of a twelve-year school: additional 200M a month. Deputy heads always earn half the additional allowance of the head.

Notes to this chapter are on p 121

10

Tertiary Education

UNIVERSITIES

THERE are six universities in the GDR, located in Berlin, Leipzig, Halle, Jena, Rostock and Greifswald and, in addition, the technical university in Dresden. Some bear the name of a distinguished philosopher, writer or thinker, not necessarily that of the founder.

Thus the university in Berlin was founded in 1809 as the Friedrich Wilhelm University: today it bears the name of Wilhelm von Humboldt, the diplomat, humanist and philologist (one of the first men to be interested in the Basque language) who with Fichte, its first rector, and Hegel made its name world famous. It teaches philosophy, maths/science, law, economics, education, theology, medicine, veterinary science, agriculture, horticulture, forestry. Of its 22,000 students, 51 per cent come from working-class homes; 11,200 are day students; 10,000 are in adult and further education, the rest in research.

Leipzig University, which became the Karl-Marx University in 1953, was founded in 1409 with a nucleus of 400 German students who split off from their Czech fellow-students in the University of Prague—on which it was modelled. It specialises in philosophy, philology, maths/science, agriculture, law, economics, theology, medicine, veterinary science and journalism.

Halle University is today the Martin Luther University. It was founded in 1694 by the Elector of Brandenburg, Frederick III, afterwards king of Prussia, and was traditionally the home of Protestant theology. Jena University, inaugurated in 1558, had Hegel, Fichte, Schlegel and Schiller on its staff in the eighteenth century. It was from this university that Karl Marx received his doctor's degree in 1841. The University of Rostock was founded in 1410 and twice in its history it moved away, to Greifswald in 1437 and to Bützow in 1760. The smallest university, that of Greifswald, founded in 1456, is today the Ernst Moritz Arndt University and teaches philosophy, maths/science, medicine and theology.

These six universities were, until 1933, places of learning in the great European tradition enjoying freedom of teaching and research. In a different category was the one-time College of Dresden, founded in 1890 and now the technical university. It now deals with maths/science, building sciences, mechanical engineering, technology, electrical engineering, economics of engineering, polytechnical education and cultural studies.

POST-WAR REFORMS

Post-war changes, referred to as tertiary education reforms, came in waves. In 1945–6, when school staffs were purged and the schools opened to all comers, there was also a widening of entry to make university education accessible to any who had the ability to take advantage of it. Worker and peasant faculties were opened as a three-year bridge to university courses for those inadequately prepared to proceed to them immediately. These are now no longer needed and have been disbanded. Such faculties were an innovation to which the traditional German professor, jealous for the standards of his institution, did not take kindly. There were wholesale voluntary or compulsory retirements of university teachers. An instance was the first post-war rector of Jena, Professor Hund, a distinguished scientist, who resigned from office when he was ordered to restrict his normal intake to 60 per cent and devote 40 per cent of the places available to candidates who were to take the pre-university course in a worker/peasant faculty. In the interests of learning and a care

G

for standards, he refused to believe that inadequate early schooling could be overcome by any bridge courses. He maintained
that such students could never rise to the challenge of the university, and in defence of his ideas pointed out that the doors
of the university had never been closed on those who could
make their way regardless of their social origins.

The second wave of reform (1950–1) extended the academic
year to ten months, introduced basic philosophy for all and insisted on practical work in industry or agriculture for every
student. But the universities themselves had changed in character. They were no longer places for the dilettante student who
could take as long as he liked over his university course. They
first provided everything by abolishing fees, and then they expected from the beneficiaries, most of whom received maintenance grants, a definite return to society. Because of this ex-
pectation the state, up to 1961, viewed with disquiet any indications of a brain-drain to West Germany and indeed to any
western countries.

The idea is sometimes floated abroad today that preference in
the GDR is given to children of working-class origin, over children from other backgrounds; this is untrue. But the working
man's child with the ability to study can do so free of financial
anxiety, thanks to adequate state provision.

Until the Tertiary Education Reform in 1968 the universities
were structured, as they had traditionally been, into faculties,
each with a dean and a faculty board. Professors alone sat on the
senate though there was student representation at faculty level
and their participation in every area of university policy-making
played a vital part in academic life. Since the Tertiary Reform
of 1968 the faculties have been abolished and universities
together with other institutes of higher education are under the
control of a Minister of Higher Education advised by a council
of fourteen members. Professors and non-professional staff are
state appointments. Though the offices of rector and pro-rector
remain, together with the college council which is the highest

university body, in the place of faculties there are now sections unifying university and institute, each with a director (appointed for three years by the rector); within the sections, university and institute professors, teachers and students work as co-partners on common tasks in the area of agreed research and on projects designed to further GDR industries. The university takes responsibility for research and research designs: it is not simply an auxiliary of industry. Former deans of faculties and directors of institutes most frequently become leaders of research groups.

The underlying ideas of the reform were to simplify structures, facilitate communication and cross-fertilisation, further team work, eliminate overlap and raise the general level of research planned up to the year 2000.

Instead of the senate there is an *advisory council*, nominated by the rector, on which there is strong student representation, as well as representation of scientific assistants and workers from associated plants. Instead of faculty boards, there is a *scientific council* on which only university teachers and students may sit: it is solely concerned with research work. From the outset professors, lecturers and students regard themselves as equally responsible for all that happens in tertiary education.

ENTRANCE REQUIREMENTS AND COURSES

There is no general problem about entrance to higher education since there are enough places to meet demands. The entrance requirements are the possession of the *Abitur* and the satisfactory completion of a year of social service. The final classes of the extended secondary school are very much under the eye of their future teachers and once the students are in tertiary education the drop-out rate is low, because the staffing ratio is high and students can get all the help they need.

The first two years of university work are devoted to subjects based on curricula evolved in 1968. Such areas might be biology/chemistry; German studies/history; Slavonic studies/French; maths/physics. Teaching is by lecture (normally ninety minutes long) and seminar, and very gifted students may work on an individual syllabus. Attendance is compulsory and the student is regarded as responsible for himself. The end-of-year examinations decide the fitness of a student to continue his studies; it is generally agreed that those who have no serious purpose in study of a scientific nature at this level have no place here.

Every student, whatever his discipline, has to study Russian and one other foreign language for two years. This means that many students will have done, in all, nine years of Russian. The amount required outside the philosophy section is mainly a reading knowledge of the literature of the special subject and the ability to speak of it in simple terms with foreign guests.

Every student has to study Marxism-Leninism also. In the imposing entrance to the Humboldt University, at the head of the staircase, is a copy of the Communist Manifesto as the 'Hohelied des Marxismus' and high above it a quotation from Karl Marx: 'Philosophers have only interpreted the world in different ways; it is up to men to change it.' The order of subjects listed in a timetable for students of the Protestant faculty of theology (1965–6) gave a further indication of the importance attached to the state philosophy.

Basic studies	*per week*
Political economy	2 hours
History of working class movement	3 hours
Historical materialism	2 hours
Special lectures on political clericalism	2 hours
Special subjects	*per week*
Philosophy	5½ hours
Old Testament	7½ hours
New Testament	17½ hours
Church history	13½ hours
Dogmatic theology	14 hours
Moral theology	13 hours[1]

Every student is also expected to engage actively in physical education and to engage in some form of social work.

Use is made of handouts of data that are time-wasting to take down in notes, of some programming and of cybernetics; students are gradually initiated into research procedures. In the last two years there is specialisation in team research, with projects and practical work that can be used in plants, agricultural enterprises or in social institutions. The idea of the function of the university as an agency for teaching and research is still operative, but research is no longer pure but applied research, functional, and often financed from outside the university.

EXAMINATIONS AND POSTGRADUATE WORK

The diploma at the end of the four years of study is a state examination, both written and practical, with a submission of the student's own contribution to the research of his year.

Those judged proficient enough may spend another two to three years in research, studying for their doctorate: permanent researchers are trained through research, as are future university teachers.

Despite pressure of work, the postgraduate student is not allowed to live in an ivory tower away from the realities of life. He is usually a member of the Free German Youth and does some social work.

GRANTS AND CONDITIONS

Some 82 per cent of students get maintenance grants of up to 190M a month, with an increment rewarding outstanding work, the ordinary grant decreasing as the parents' combined income increases. Married students are judged to be independent of each other and of their parents and get 190M each a month, without reference to parental means. Similarly students from homes with four or more children get the full grant, whatever the parents' income. Students studying theology get grants like everyone else.

Students who fall ill and are unable to work get 90 per cent of their grant for a full year, or if they are hospital cases, for half a year. There is no embargo on summer vacation work and the student is paid the rate for the job.

Research students receive 300M a month in their first year; 350M in their second year; 450M in their third year.

Hostel fees are 10M a month for a room and canteen meals are cheap, 60Pf to 1M. Something like 65 per cent of all students live in hostels where the warden has overall responsibility for their work, social and political awareness, morality and physical welfare. He also controls the finances of the hostel.

About 75 per cent of students attend lectures in full daytime study, and attending lectures means 100 per cent attendance. Some 23 per cent work through correspondence courses and are entitled to thirty-two to fifty-two free days a year for lectures and discussions and may claim up to six months paid leave of absence from their place of work. Because they work they are normally charged fees of 120M. In addition 2 per cent of students work through evening classes. A man can be considered a student up to the age of thirty-five, or up to forty-five if he studies by correspondence.

STUDENT UNREST?

Why is there no student revolt in the GDR? It is too facile to say that it would not be allowed. The reason may be that the structures are new, not stratified, that there is effective student participation in policy-making and implementation, no gap between teacher and taught, freedom to criticise lectures with those who give them. But above all there is the responsibility of the student to society, which regards the subsidising of his education as an investment.

THE TEACHERS' CENTRES

We have seen that children are well catered for (p 71): so are their teachers.

The Berlin Teachers' Centre (the House of the Teacher) was built to replace a city teachers' club destroyed during the war.

Situated in the Alexanderplatz with fountains playing by its side, this twelve-storey building of concrete and glass, with an exterior decorative representational frieze in red and gold encircling the floors that house the book-stocks, is still imposing though it has been rather dwarfed by the TV tower and the Stadt-Berlin hotel. Like the university institutes of education in England it provides retraining, further qualifications and short courses for teachers, and at the same time functions as a graduate club and focal point for the recreational and cultural life of the teacher.

Inside there is space for exhibitions of pictures, ceramics and sculpture, a large concert hall with very modern seating, a reasonably priced café and restaurant open to the general public, rooms for various circles, clubs, lectures and discussion groups— music making, dramatics, language practice, photography, arts, crafts, radio-construction, dancing, concerts, shows of all kinds, theatre and cinema. For larger gatherings the Congress Hall, immediately next door to the Teachers' Centre, can house audiences of up to 1,000 people.

The Education Library housed in the Centre is both general and specialised, lending and reference. There are more than half a million books on loan and a large staff to help not only the teachers of Berlin and the surrounding district but also the foreign research workers to whom its facilities are readily extended. Here are all the adjuncts of an up-to-date library, including micro-films, slides and an efficient cataloguing system.

Courses for systematic further study can be pursued here, and teachers' conferences and short courses are held in collaboration with tertiary-level lecturers. Every need of the teacher in service, the parent and the school-leaver is catered for. There is tuition and coaching for those who need it. The whole building is also a central meeting ground where teachers can exchange ideas and get professional help, as in the English 'workshops' provided by city or university as a meeting ground for schoolteachers where books, tapes, illustrations can be examined away from the atmosphere of school. In East Germany teachers can bring their families along too, for dances, concerts and meals. The degree of refinement, the care of the building, the spotless cleanliness and the fine modern furnishings are in the best German tradition. And just as children meet distinguished artists, musicians, and performers in the Pioneer Palaces, so do the teachers in the Teachers' Centre. The building is open on every weekday from 8 am to 10 pm and on Sunday evenings to all who have a right to use it. This verification of credentials takes place equally at all official buildings, as in England and elsewhere.

And Berlin is not the only city with such a centre. There is one in each central town of the region, though these are more modest. The newest is the fine one in Halle, opened in 1971 under its first Director, Herr Walther Obst.

Notes for this chapter are on p 122

11

Educational Research and Book Provision

THE PEDAGOGICAL CONGRESS

A PEDAGOGICAL CONGRESS is held at five-yearly intervals in the GDR to review the achievements of the previous year, and to consider foreseeable and mandatory development within every area of education. The first such congress took place in Berlin in August 1945 for the whole of Germany; the last, the seventh, was held in the GDR between 5 and 7 May 1970.

Unlike educational bodies that make recommendations which appear to go unheeded or are only partially implemented, the Congress sets fresh or intensified norms for the years ahead to all concerned with education at all levels. By 1 September 1970 all the directives issued by the seventh congress were in operation or in the course of being implemented.

At this congress, prepared over a period of six months, there were papers, debates and discussions not only among experts but among teachers, students, pupils, parents and members of the general public. As they met under the motto 'We teach and learn in the spirit of Lenin', it would not be inaccurate to say that its thinking was definitely communistic. There were two principal speakers, the Minister of Education and the Chairman of the People's Party. And taking part in the debate were thirty-six foreign delegates (from the Soviet Union, Poland, Czechoslovakia, Hungary, Bulgaria, Rumania, Yugoslavia), together with the political, educational and industrial, trade union and civic representatives of the Republic, and headmasters, teachers, pupils, researchers and scientists.

The Minister of Education Margot Honecker, after reviewing past educational achievement in the Republic, roundly asserted that 'there was and is no ideology-free education, no education without a sense of values. It does not exist in capitalism and certainly not in socialism.'[1] Consequently people who claimed that they would see eye to eye, educationally, with the GDR if the ideology could be put on one side were asking for the impossible. In defining polytechnical education the minister made the important point that it is not vocational education, neither is it a substitute for vocational education though it provides essential bases for future vocational activity, nor, she concluded, has it 'anything in common with indifferent technical teaching'.

In connection with educational development for the next five years the following objectives were announced:

1. An increase in the number and scope of electives in the extended secondary school.

2. The consistent raising of standards and an increase in the number of options in vocational schools to make them, in their own right, as good as the extended secondary schools and not watered-down versions of them.

3. A psychological study to be made of what is implied in the term 'socialist personality', as distinct from 'individuality' in capitalist nations, a conception she described as 'being your own neighbour'.

4. Research into ways and means of improving the education of the handicapped.

Not a single sector of education, nor a single group of people actively or incidentally concerned with education was overlooked; to everyone came the challenge to surpass present achievement. By the autumn every sector had its plans worked out—small wonder that education in the GDR is a dynamic, constantly improving, changing thing. At this Congress there were 245 contributions from the floor, made by all sorts of people: administrators, teachers, managers, working men, pupils. This is good evidence that education is important to all and the concern of all.

THE ACADEMY OF PEDAGOGICAL SCIENCES

The German Academy of Pedagogical Sciences was the title conferred in September 1970 on the German Central Pedagogical Institute in Berlin, but whereas the latter was concerned only with work at school level, as an academy it extends its field to all education. It is the central research body for the whole of the Republic, working in close co-operation with the Ministry of Education and, inter alia, researching into problems discussed at the Pedagogical Congress. At its head is a director appointed by the Ministry, and under him are deputies, each responsible for one main section.

Its various departments deal with all theoretical aspects of education; with various levels of education and curriculum development; with polytechnical education; with all aspects of educational documentation; with the economics of education; with teaching materials; with the special problems of the Sorb bilingual area (the minority on the Czech border). Their experiments are tested in selected schools and institutes and their findings are submitted to the Ministry and, if approved, passed through various appropriate channels to the particular groups concerned. The academy also has research problems referred to it by the Ministry. Research workers from the Max-Planck Institute (West Berlin) specially detailed to study East German education, have for years been going over to East Berlin to discuss research findings and there is also a considerable body of comparative research done in other places in West Germany.[2]

THE GERMAN STATE LIBRARY

The most important library, the German State Library, is one of the great collections of the world, comparable with the British

Museum and the Bibliothèque Nationale in Paris. It had its beginnings in 1661 as the private collection of the Elector Frederick of Brandenburg, and was housed in Cologne-on-the-Spree, then north of Berlin but now part of it. Access to this valuable collection of 2,000 books was at first restricted to members of the royal family and to scholars of standing. But by 1740 the number of books had swelled with the addition of forty other collections to 72,000 volumes, and in the reign of Frederick II the library was transferred to a building of its own near the Royal Opera House. The quarters were cramped, there was no general catalogue but only the separate listings of the five main categories of books, so that using the library was a very complicated operation.

The opening of the Humboldt University in 1810 provided more space for books and made it possible to reorganise the State Library. Between 1811 and 1827 a first alphabetical catalogue was made. The nineteenth century brought an accretion of private collections, MSS and autographs, until the library building was again too small to cope with its own riches. In 1903, a new Royal Library was begun in *Unter den Linden* not far from the university library and that of the German Academy of Sciences; it was a thirteen-storeyed building with a courtyard and fountains and built in that massive style so characteristic of Prussian official architecture. Badly damaged in World War II, it was repaired and in part reopened in 1946, though some of its treasures had been dispersed.

Today it has a general director and two directors (one of whom is a woman) and a staff of 500, of whom 150 are highly qualified scholars. Its areas of specialisation are (a) music, (b) MSS and literary archives including a copy of the Gutenberg Bible and a large collection of autographs of monarchs, famous public men, writers and musicians, (c) early printed books, (d) cartography, (e) a children's and young people's library. It has close links with other Berlin libraries, with those of Potsdam and Dresden and with the inter-library loan service.

As in the British Museum, reference works are on open shelves, but in Berlin they are arranged, according to their category, in separate reading rooms where periodicals are also on display. But, unlike the British Museum, there is a lending section. Users come with a recommendation from an educational institution, a works, a social organisation and are issued with a daily or a yearly ticket for which a minimal fee is payable. There is also a scheme of corporate membership, whereby a subscription paid by an institution entitles its members to become users of the library.

At the moment the library is bringing its catalogue up to date.

PUBLIC LIBRARIES

The city library in Berlin is a prototype, on a larger scale, of the 17,190 public libraries in the Republic. It was founded in 1907 and extended and housed in a splendid new building in 1966. There were then 987,000 volumes and 1,400,000 is the target for 1975. Behind the pewter decorated gate which features the letter A in 119 alphabets is a reference and lending library in modern style for users aged fourteen and upwards. Excluding the administrative, technical and auxiliary personnel, the library is manned by a staff of 160; 24 are highly qualified librarians, 16 are scholars, 120 are librarians with a particular area of specialisation. Librarians, of whom two-thirds are women, can start at sixteen and study by correspondence, or begin after a four-year university course.

The locale has all the features of a very up-to-date library: plenty of space, excellent accommodation in a room with 220 reading places, an open-air reading room for use in fine weather, automatic lockers for cases and personal possessions, and an efficient electric chute system for request and delivery of books from the stocks. Another notable feature is a big music section with records, six record players and kiosks and listening facilities for jazz, classical music and songs of all kinds from all countries.

The number of young readers shows a marked upward trend

accounted for by the increased reading demanded by revised school syllabuses, by conducted tours of the library for school-children of eight to eleven, and by co-operation between the local education authority and the director of the library.

SPECIALIST LIBRARIES

For the special needs of readers from science and technical insti-tutes there are two specialist libraries, one in Berlin and the other in Leipzig. These collections are mainly for people engaged in research at the highest level. Other libraries in other towns are geared to special needs, like the pedagogical libraries found in every town, which bring together specialist-subject and educa-tional books which teachers need for teaching and study, and volumes of general cultural interest, together with the entire range of educational periodicals produced in the Republic. Libraries catering for specific professional interests are housed in the related institutes.

LIBRARY TRAINING

There is a library institute for the training of scientific and technical librarians in Berlin, and since 1971 the library institute in Leipzig has had the responsibility of training all-round librarians and of providing a correspondence course in scientific and technical librarianship.

BOOK PROVISION

Book provision, other than school textbooks, in 1969 amounted to 113,980 volumes. New titles numbered 5,169 as against 4,809 in 1955. Among these new titles it is interesting to note that the largest number (999) were in belles lettres, the lowest in housecraft (30). Other titles include:

Religion and theology	282
Philosophy and psychology	77
Law	64
Social studies and statistics	141

SCHOOL BOOKS

One of the biggest publishing firms, the *Volk u. Wissen Verlag* in Berlin (see also p 26), is nationally owned and is concerned only with the production of books and papers for teachers and for schoolchildren of all ages for school work, reference and recreational reading. Atlases and encyclopaedias, however, are produced by the firm *Zeit im Bild* in Dresden. The Berlin firm produces on an average 200 new titles a year and in all has about 25 million copies in circulation. Textbooks have to be renewed roughly every four or five years, and at these periods changes can be made. Production at present takes up to eighteen months but serious efforts are being made to reduce this to twelve months. Authors may submit manuscripts on their own initiative or may do so by invitation; alternatively a team works together on a book. Teachers' collectives submit their ideas about new methods and these are given due consideration. Everyone who works on the editorial staff has been a teacher, and the editorial board consists of practising teachers, researchers and regional advisers. The contributors to the various teaching subjects magazines are teachers, the editorial staff and academics invited by the publishers.

Printing is sent out to some hundred different printing and binding firms and if any firm fails to fulfil a contract the work is transferred elsewhere. In the early days the books were cheaply printed on very grey and unattractive paper. Today, better paper, binding and colour processes are used. All this increases the price. Parents pay for school books according to their means, some paying the whole cost and some nothing at all. There is one textbook containing the minimum assignment for each year in each subject. It is designed to be within the compass of the average child and to be used as a starting point for the more able.

Notes for this section are on p 122

12

Some Figures and Conclusions

EXPENDITURE ON EDUCATION

IT is extremely difficult in looking at statements of official expenditure on education in a socialist country to estimate what percentage of the gross national product is devoted to education. Queries about this invariably produce the answer that finance is very complicated because money comes to educational institutions not only from the ministry which pays the salaries but from the region that puts up the schools, the local council that pays for their day-to-day running, and from factories, which are wholly reponsible for their own factory-schools (though not for the salaries of the teacher) and partly responsible for the schools of which they are the patrons. Groups of parents, individuals or firms also provide unpaid labour for supplying and installing equipment or laying out grounds and so on.

The USA Office of Education, in a communication to the present writer in 1971, estimated that in 1963 the GDR devoted 6 per cent of its national income to education (UNESCO data). There appear to be no published percentages for the GDR for the following year. It is calculated that the GDR today spends some 8·1 per cent of its national budget on education: the percentage of the gross national product would be lower.

Figures for various forms of expenditure can be found in the Statistical Year Book of the GDR (1970), but since a number of items are grouped together it is difficult to make accurate deductions. In the year 1969, the amount spent by the state on all forms of education, including vocational and technical schools and sport as well as pre-school and compulsory school age groups, was 4,498,214M million.

Allocations to pre-primary institutions amounted to 394,549,000M, of which 386,174,000M was for nursery schools; 161,991,000M was spent on children's homes and work centres; 1,915,514,000M on day and boarding schools; 85,535,000M on institutes, area offices and inservice training; 309,809,000M on school and children's meals, 49,777,000M on Pioneer houses, stations and camps; 48,946,000M on holiday homes. The sum of 848,876,000M for vocational education was distributed as follows:

625,152,000M for factory schools (a charge now withdrawn)
102,281,000M for vocational schools and hostels in rural areas
70,822,000M for workers' faculties (now closed)

The 313,830,000M reserved for technical schools included

32,144,000M for hostels and maintenance grants
123,011,000M for sports provision, including both installations and equipment

On science in its widest sense 2,26,932,000M was spent.

720,881,000M for universities and tertiary-level institutes
65,795,000M for hostels and meals (where provided)
434,153,000M for scientific technical institutes
339,503,000M for other scientific expenditure

There is no means of estimating relative charges on state and local funds for 1969. The only available figures relate to 1954 when current expenditure on education was 2,985,335,000M, of which 1,555,003,000M was centrally and 1,430,332,000M was locally provided.

SCHOOLS AND PUPILS

In 1969 the number of nursery schools, day and weekly, was 10,854.

Number of places in them   542,693
Nursery school staff   39,698
Percentage of children in nursery schools   55·4
    (this percentage to be raised to 70 by 1975)

Numbers in nursery schools:

    2,786 classes have up to 12 children
    10,604 classes have 13–18 children
    18,771 classes have 19+ children

The number of polytechnical schools was 7,764.

10 year polytechnical schools   6,923
Pupils per class   27·7
        (Berlin 31·8, Neubrandenburg 25·7)

The number of special schools was 537.

Pupils per class   13·1
  (Suhl 14·8, the highest; Neubrandenburg 11·5, the lowest)

The number of extended secondary schools was 304.

Number of pupils   51,923
Pupils per class   25·0
Abitur candidates from the extended secondary
  school as against 19,678 in 1955   23,943

The number of vocational schools was 1,153.

General schools   391
Factory schools   705
Medical schools   57
Pupils per class   22·4

Skilled workers taking qualifying examinations numbered
240,811.

55,749 in agriculture, horticulture, forestry, fishing
 2,369 in mining, masonry, ceramics, glass
16,647 in building, carpentry, manufacture
62,601 in metal production and manufacture, electrotechnics,
  electronics
 5,076 in chemistry, plastics
 5,220 in paper production and manufacture, printing trades
10,848 in textiles and leather

7,049 in food trade and luxury goods
7,812 in various technical trades, machinists
67,441 in various other categories of retail trade, hotel work, etc
(there are in all 61 named categories)

CONCLUSIONS

When one tries to give an objective but kaleidoscopic idea of a new type of education one is sometimes faced with the criticism (voiced usually by teachers rather than by students): 'I expect you were shown only the best.' All countries show off their best, but in the GDR I was able to choose what I wanted to see, modify any proposed programme, talk to very many officials, headmasters, professors, teachers, and voice all the doubts, queries and criticisms I liked. I was shown teaching of varying degrees of efficiency from the brilliant to the mediocre, and that in all subjects on the timetable. I could of course use libraries at will and wander about freely and unaccompanied in every town I visited.

To claim that this new and interesting conception of German education, born only in the middle of this century, has already achieved 100 per cent success would be absurd, since the system is under constant review. The fact that at teachers' gatherings, at the Pedagogical Congress and in private conversation the admission is made that there is still a long road to travel may serve to counteract any impression that the GDR is satisfied with every aspect of the educational system.

The main achievement has been the creation of a type of education new to German thinking and that at a time of extreme national depression born of defeat and of fear of the future. Fifty years previously the USSR had had to cope with a very different problem when the very rudiments of education had to be given to large numbers of illiterate people. By 1940, however, the educational drives in the Union were beginning to bear fruit, and when the moment came for Germans to re-think their educational system there was some help available for them in achieving a socialist formula; but this they did on German lines and with German efficiency and drive.

The claim that from 1945 German education took a new road is amply justified. The turning of a whole nation into working men and women created an ambience in which the socialist school could work. It is quite a usual thing for the trade of a teacher or an official to be referred to publicly—for instance, the caption to a 1970 photograph of the Minister of Defence chatting informally with the men of a tank corps includes the information that he was a fitter by trade. The idea of equal opportunity for all children has been made a reality. There is only one system of education and no means of contracting out of it with money. The building up of an almost wholly new teaching force to meet the new conditions created in 1945 was in itself a tremendous achievement and an act of faith, and like all such acts, it was tried and probably strengthened by opposition. Many thinkers concerned with mass education have believed in the formula of manual work allied with intellectual work and offset by aesthetic and other interests. The GDR has realised this alliance more effectively than the USSR. She has worked out the theory and practice of polytechnical education and its social consequences. But she has done much more than that. In science and technology and also in linguistics, both theoretical and applied, she holds her place in Europe.

Notes

Chapter 1 SOME ASPECTS OF THE GDR

1   The figures are the latest available, taken from the *Staatistisches Jahrbuch* (1970).

2   In the summer of 1948 the four-power Control Council came to an end and West Berlin began to play its troubled part as a bastion in the Cold War. In reply to the unification of the three western zones, the Soviet zone became the German Democratic Republic on 7 October 1949. Even today, in 1972, its existence is not recognised by Great Britain; for a long time the Federal Republic hoped that a united Germany was possible. That hope has been abandoned. In the *Bulletin* of the Press and Information of the FRG (18 no 4, 1971, 1–2) Herr W. Brandt is reported as saying what the history of the last twenty-five years has progressively confirmed: 'We must recognise that the reunification of Germany in the original sense is no longer possible . . . The term unification stems from the time directly after World War II. Until somewhere in the mid 1950s, it seemed still to be possible on the basis of free elections to reunite the parts of Germany that had been separated from each other by the occupying powers. That would have required an agreement between the three Western powers and the Soviet Union. Such a happy solution of the German question was not achieved . . . In Germany two states with quite different political and social systems have come into existence, systems that do not led themselves easily to reunification.'

3   Its composition at present is:
       56·6 per cent working men
       14·0 per cent office workers
       11·8 per cent artisans and business people
       10·4 per cent farmers

4·6 per cent intellectuals
2·6 per cent others

4 Cf the city of Strasbourg's reparation gift of the Synagogue of
   Peace to the Jewish community after the war.

Chapter 2 HISTORICAL RETROSPECT

1 For the history of education in Germany before 1945 see Samuel,
   R. H., & Hinton, Thomas R. *Education and Society in Modern
   Germany* (1948).
2 Cf Feis, H. *Between War and Peace* (1960).
3 Supplement to the *Gazette of the Control Commission*, no 18.
4 *The German Tribune* (14 October 1971), 1.
5 Text of agreement in Supplement no 1 to the *Gazette of the
   Control Commission*, 13 et seq.
6 Official Bulletin of the Allied Command, Berlin, no 8 (September
   1947, BK/o(47)/205).
7 The inception of the German Communist Party, the Spartacus
   Group, 1918–19, had roughly coincided with educational and
   other innovations in the Soviet Union. The study of great
   educators of the past, the aspiration towards a school linked with,
   rather than divorced from, life, a classless, politically controlled
   school—all this came into Communist thinking. They were
   realistic enough to know that such a school was a non-starter so
   long as outside its walls class divisions destroyed the conception
   of oneness that could be operative in it. But the party was in no
   position to press its claims at a period when the future of the
   USSR itself was uncertain. In 1930 they were again considering
   the role of the school but as soon as Hitler came to power in
   1933, Communists were relieved of their teaching functions and
   exiled or imprisoned.
8 Samuel, R. H., & Hinton, Thomas R. *Education and Society in
   Modern Germany* (1948), 173–4. 'It would be mistaken to regard
   the school reforms in the Russian zone as merely the implementation of an alien system, though it does reflect to a certain extent
   the principles underlying educational organisation in Russia. It
   may be said to be a development out of many of the best features of
   the theory and practice of German education in the past, in
   particular of the "Einheitsschule" (comprehensive school) as
   interpreted by German democrats . . . Certainly, the curricula
   worked out by German educationalists in the zone reveal a re-

markable breadth of mind and they successfully follow the principle of integrated instruction.'

9   Quoted from a copy in the State and Law Library at Potsdam, Babelsberg, and at length because of the difficulty of locating the document (author's translation).

10 From 1956, 6–16.

11 The suppression of confessional schools was an aspect of Soviet thinking which the West, with a different ethic, deplored as atheistic humanism in action; moreover, anything that put Communism in a position of strength roused grave concern.

12 In the foreword to *Soviet Education*, 13 nos 3–4 (January–February 1971), the editors use the expression 'the failure of the polytechnical experiment in secondary schooling' and a Soviet teacher in 1971, in answer to a question put by teachers from many other nations, replied 'I'm afraid that polytechnical education was only a dream.'

13 It is further interesting to note that in her *'Bildungskatastrophe'*, Federal Germany has adopted some of the educational ideas of the GDR and that only tentatively have some English Schools of Education considered the training of headmasters and educational administrators.

Chapter 3   THE EDUCATIONAL SYSTEM AND PRE-SCHOOL INSTITUTIONS

1   GDR official English translation of the Constitution with minor emendations for greater clarity.

Chapter 4   POLYTECHNICAL EDUCATION

1   *Education and Training in the GDR*, State Publishing House (1966), 86.

2   Ibid, 89. The outstanding success of the GDR in European games and international events may well be attributed to the general policy of disciplined physical education.

3   Cf article 'Foreign Languages in the GDR' by Mina J. Moore-Rinvolucri in *Modern Languages*, XLVII no 2 (June 1966), 66–9.

4   Kienitz, W., et al. *Einheitlichkeit und Differenzierung*, Volk und Wissen Verlag, Berlin (1971), 316.

5   There are 84 special establishments for sport and for music with 32,147 pupils.

Chapter 5 BEYOND COMPULSORY SCHOOLING

1   With the gigantic Leuna complex is linked the Halle-Neustadt
    trading estate, conceived in 1961, begun in 1967 and now in
    phase four of its completion. It is within a tram-ride of the
    parent-city and is provided with everything that could make for
    contented living: a stadium, clubs, restaurants, a cinema, baths,
    markets, a kindergarten, schools. The houses are in flats of one
    to four rooms and there is a block of old people's flats for the firm's
    retired workers. Heavy traffic is excluded from the town.

Chapter 6 THE DISADVANTAGED CHILD

1   See the present author's forthcoming article on 'Hypnopaedia or
    natural sleep learning of modern languages' in the *Journal of the
    Teachers of Russian* (1973).

Chapter 7 YOUTH CLUBS AND MOVEMENTS

1   Ernst Thälmann was a Communist who died in the concentra-
    tion camp of Buchenwald, Weimar, and whose permanently
    flower-heaped gravestone is honoured there.
2   Grant, Nigel. *Soviet Education*, Pelican (1968), 48.
3   *Sozialistiches Bildungsrecht:* Staatsverlag der DDR, 1968, Sec
    167.

Chapter 9 TEACHERS AND THEIR TRAINING

1   A copy of the institute's booklet *Anleitung zum Einführungs-
    praktikum an Instituten für Lehrerbildung* (Institut für Lehrerbil-
    dung, Halle, 65pp), is given both to the student and to the
    school.
2   Erfurt has 1,800 full-time students and 1,000 students studying
    by correspondence. There are 300 assistants and 200 professors
    and lecturers on the staff.
3   Holidays are: autumn 6 days; Christmas 12 days; February/
    March 12 days; Easter 7 days; Whitsun 5 days; summer up to
    51 days.

Chapter 10 TERTIARY EDUCATION

1   It is patent that the subjects in this group are spread out over
the years of the course. The hours represent lectures and seminars.

Chapter 11 EDUCATIONAL RESEARCH AND BOOK PROVISION

1   *vii Pädagogischer Kongress der DDR* (1970), Staatsverlag der
DDR, Berlin (1970), 41.
2   Subert, H. *Bildungspraxis in Deutschland BRD und DDR im
Vergleich*, Bertelsmann Universitätsverlag, Düsseldorf, and many
other similar studies.

Appendix

Students at tertiary level studying for a first qualification

Discipline	Totals			Of these					
				In taught courses			In correspondence courses		
	Students	1st Year	Finals	Students	1st Year	Finals	Students	1st Year	Finals
Mathematics/natural sciences	10,072	2,904	1,261	9,293	2,801	1,158	609	78	77
Mathematics	2,560	881	210	2,548	881	210	11	—	—
Physics	2,216	602	319	2,128	504	285	88	8	34
Chemistry	3,608	1,028	507	3,088	936	443	351	67	38
Biology	677	202	60	669	202	60	8	—	—
Geology	344	58	101	344	58	101	—	—	—
Geography	60	20	11	60	20	11	—	—	—
Psychology	607	113	53	456	110	48	151	3	5
Technical sciences	36,442	12,869	3,885	26,708	10,069	2,976	7,579	2,788	678
Mechanical engineering	15,434	4,896	1,683	10,885	3,736	1,269	3,357	1,157	289
Materials engineering	919	268	199	564	200	106	355	68	93
Transport engineering	2,456	1,082	238	1,837	969	198	220	108	15
Electrical engineering	11,701	4,362	1,054	8,743	3,302	823	2,426	1,056	173
Structural engineering	4,037	1,486	529	3,062	1,145	456	943	341	50
Architecture	560	135	30	560	135	30	—	—	—
Traffic engineering	509	239	43	369	196	27	140	43	16
Surveying	255	50	26	202	49	23	53	1	3
Mining engineering	221	42	83	138	28	44	85	14	39
Medical/agricultural sciences	16,548	3,160	3,668	14,769	2,844	3,310	1,779	316	358
Medicine	9,429	1,629	2,403	9,429	1,629	2,403	—	—	—
Pharmacy	589	152	186	547	151	143	42	1	43
Agricultural engineering (plant production)	2,577	396	466	1,599	268	289	978	128	177

Agricultural engineering (animal husbandry)	2,978	561	485	2,257	409	351	721	152	134
Soil engineering	324	194	23	322	194	23	2	—	—
Forestry	178	41	37	177	41	37	1	—	—
Food engineering	473	187	68	438	152	64	35	35	4
Social sciences	17,680	5,675	2,470	7,937	3,027	978	8,385	2,170	910
Political economy	4,151	905	431	1,811	603	117	2,275	302	254
Business science/economics engineering	11,630	3,708	1,841	5,073	1,899	780	5,361	1,433	634
Economic, cybernetic and organisation sciences	1,899	1,062	198	1,053	525	81	749	435	22
Philosophical, historical, political and legal sciences	5,341	1,483	582	2,237	675	237	3,104	808	345
Philosophical sciences	444	72	63	144	3	24	300	69	39
Historical sciences	296	75	46	79	12	12	217	63	34
Political and social sciences	195	—	—	63	—	—	132	—	—
Legal sciences	4,051	1,267	454	1,596	591	182	2,455	676	272
Information, documentation and library sciences	160	55	8	160	55	8	—	—	—
Regional sciences	195	14	11	195	14	11	—	—	—
Cultural, artistic and sports sciences	2,450	548	406	1,364	336	258	1,077	207	148
Cultural sciences	486	85	71	120	34	14	357	46	57
Music sciences	35	10	8	35	10	8	—	—	—
Art subjects	43	3	8	43	3	8	—	—	—
Theatre sciences	54	—	—	54	—	—	—	—	—
Sports sciences	1,295	317	196	575	156	105	720	161	91
Theology	537	133	123	537	133	123	—	—	—
Literature and linguistic sciences	1,160	344	210	843	277	164	274	67	46

Students at tertiary level studying for a first qualification

Discipline	Totals			Of these					
				In taught courses			In correspondence courses		
	Students	1st Year	Finals	Students	1st Year	Finals	Students	1st Year	Finals
General philological sciences	62	11	4	62	11	4	—	—	—
German studies	24	—	16	24	—	16	—	—	—
Slavonic studies	55	1	12	28	1	12	—	—	—
English studies	2	—	—	2	—	—	—	—	—
Romance studies	13	—	7	13	—	7	—	—	—
Other philological sciences	15	3	—	15	3	—	—	—	—
Translators for Slavonic languages	205	89	21	189	89	21	16	—	—
English	81	32	32	74	32	32	7	—	—
Romance languages	92	20	17	92	20	17	—	—	—
Other languages	38	12	—	38	12	—	—	—	—
Journalism	573	176	101	306	109	55	251	67	46
Art subjects	1,910	449	294	1,504	311	226	232	82	25
Music	664	109	145	428	30	84	62	23	—
Display	434	130	61	377	130	54	57	—	7
Applied arts	534	106	54	478	104	54	56	2	—
Plastic arts	207	47	54	207	47	34	—	—	—
Writing	71	57	34	14	—	—	57	57	—
Pedagogical studies	31,187	8,704	6,492	23,154	6,693	4,833	8,007	2,006	1,627
Teachers for comprehensive polytechnical secondary schools including extended secondary schools	27,920	7,470	5,574	20,610	5,730	4,067	7,304	1,740	1,507

Of these:

Maths/natural sciences	11,018	2,812	2,072	7,884	2,173	1,426	3,133	639	646
Polytechnics	1,728	461	463	1,728	461	463	—	—	—
History/civics	2,903	933	473	1,769	557	306	1,134	376	167
Art/music	1,660	442	386	1,408	338	281	247	104	105
Physical education	2,598	694	553	1,944	551	401	654	143	152
German	3,656	966	821	2,475	713	600	1,181	253	221
Foreign languages	4,357	1,162	806	3,402	937	590	955	225	216
Teachers for vocational, including technical, schools	1,797	408	365	1,679	407	365	118	1	—
Of these:									
Technical subjects	1,050	199	211	932	198	211	118	1	—
Medical/agricultural subjects	414	100	117	414	100	117	—	—	—
Social studies including data processing	142	34	26	142	34	26	—	—	—
Teachers for special schools and homes	474	476	337	299	299	337	175	177	—
Teachers of Marxism-Leninism	743	275	140	354	187	38	385	88	75
Pedagogical/educational sciences	43	17	45	18	17	—	25	—	45
Pioneer leaders	123	46	18	123	46	18	—	—	—
Pedagogy of music for folk music schools	87	12	13	71	7	8	—	—	—
GRAND TOTALS	122,790	36,136	19,268	87,809	27,033	14,140	31,046	8,522	4,214

Taken from the Statistical Year Book of the GDR, 1970. Apparent discrepancies in totals are accounted for by evening classes.

Selective Bibliography

English and American

Barraclough, G. *Origins of Modern Germany* (2nd ed 1947, Blackwell, Oxford)

Bodenman, P. S. *Education in the Soviet Zone of East Germany* (US Dept of Health, Education & Welfare, Bulletin 26, 1959)

Constitution of the GDR (Staatsverlag der DDR, 1968)

Education and Planning in the GDR (Staatsverlag, 1968)

Education and Training in the GDR (Staatsverlag, 1966)

Grant, N. *Society, Schools and Progress in Eastern Europe* (Pergamon, 1969)

Honecker, E. *Report of the Central Committee to the Eighth Congress of the SED* (Verlag Zeit im Bild, Dresden 1971)

How Does the GDR Solve the Problems of Higher Education? (Verlag Zeit im Bild, Dresden 1970)

Kohn, E. and Werner, O. *Teachers learn to teach* (Ministry of Education, GDR, no date)

Legun, R. *The Four-Power Agreements on Berlin* (Carl Heymann, 2nd ed, Berlin 1961)

Moore-Rinvolucri, M. J. 'East German Congress', *Bulletin of the Comparative Education Society* (July 1971), 7–8

'Foreign Languages in the German Democratic Republic', *Modern Languages* (June 1966), 66–9

'Some Aspects of Education in the German Democratic Republic', *Journal of the Institutes of Education of the Universi-*

ties of Newcastle-upon-Tyne and Durham (September 1971), 18–20

'Teachers' Centre in East Berlin', *The Times Educational Supplement* (2 August 1968), 218

Official Gazette of the Control Commission for Germany 1945, nos 1–18 (Allied Secretariat, Berlin)

Polytechnical training and education in the GDR (Ministry of Education, no date)

Wältage, H. *Student in the GDR* (Zeit im Bild, Dresden 1968)

Year Book of Education (London): *The Russian Zone of Occupation* (1948); *Higher Education in East Germany* (1957)

German sources (mainly GDR)

Ankermann, G., et al. *Lehrer u. Eltern* (Volk u. Wissen Verlag, Berlin 1968)

Becker, H., et al. *Die Zwei Entwicklungswege unserer Nation u. Ihre Widerspiegelung im Schulbuch* (Deutsches pädagogisches Zentralinstitut, Berlin, V u. W V, 1963)

Befehle der sowjetischen Militarverwaltung der Oberkommandierende der Gruppe der sowjetischen Besatzungstruppen in Deutschland

Berger, H. *Das politischorganisierte Kinderkollektiv im Erziehungsprozess* (Berlin, V u. W V, 1970)

Zur patriotischen Erziehung in der Unterstufe (Berlin, V u. W V, 1962)

Berlin Education Authority. *Das Schulgesetz für Gross-Berlin* (Magistrat für Gross-Berlin, 26 June 1948)

Deutsches Pädagogisches Zentral Institut. *Jahrbuch* v 1 and 2 (1968)

Das Schulwesen socialistischen Länder in Europa (1962)

Pädagogische Wissenschaft u. Schule (2v, 1964)

Doernberg, S. *Kurze Geschichte der DDR* (Dietz Verlag, Berlin 1965)

Dokumente zur Jugendpolitik der DDR (Staatsverlag der DDR, 1965)

Engelbert, M., et al. *Zur polytechnischen Bildung u. Erziehung in der DDR* (W Berlin: Pädagogisches Zentrum, 1969)

Ergebnisse der Einführung neuen Lehrpläne u. Lernmethoden an der 10-klassigen allgemeinbildenden polytechnischen Oberschule (Staatrat der DDR. Abt. Presse u. Information, Heft 9 1968)

Evers, C. H. *Modelle moderner Bildungspolitik* (Diesterweg 1969)

Fichtner, K. D. *Die Lernmotivation der Schüler der Kl. 9 u. 10 in Fachunterrichtsraumsystem*

Forst, W., et al. *Das Vorschulkind* (Berlin, V u. W V, 1970)

Frankiewicz, H., et al. *Polytechnische Bildung u. Erziehung in der DDR* (Berlin, V u. W V, 1967)

Friedrich, W. *Jugend Heute* (Berlin VEB Deutscher Verlag der Wissenschaften, Berlin 1966)

Gesetzblatt. (Deutscher Zentralverlag, Gmb H 1949–54)

Glowe, H., et al. *Das Sondernschulwesen der DDR* (V u. W V, Berlin 1967)

Grundsätze für die Berufsausbildung im einheitlichen sozialistischen Bildungssystem (Information des Staatrates, Heft 10 1968)

Günther, K. H. and Uhlig, G. *Geschichte der Schule in der DDR 1945 bis 1968* (V u. W V, Berlin 1969)

Haase, D., et al. *Das politisch—organisierte Kinderkollektiv im Erziehungs-prozess* (V u. W V., Berlin 1970)

Hofman, F. *Ausbildung zum Fachlehrer der 10-klassigen allgemeinbildenden polytechnischen Oberschule am Pädagogischen Institut Halle/Saale* (published by the Institute, 1970)

Kienitz, W. *Einheitlichkeit u. Differenzierung im Bildungswesen* (V u. W V, Berlin 1971)

Krahn, H. and Rückert, G. *Sozialistisches Bildungsrecht* (V u. W V, Berlin 1968)

Lehrmaterial für das Lehrmeisterfernstudium. Didaktik 1–3 (Lehrmeister-Institut, Karl-Marx-Stadt 1965)

Lompscher, J. and Reischock, W. *Die Bewältigung der Zukunft* (V u. W V, Berlin 1966)

Marx/Engels über Erziehung und Bildung (V u. W V, Berlin 1960)

Melchert, et al. *Zur wissenschaftlichen Leitung der Bildungs-und-Erziehungs-arbeit* (V u. W. V, Berlin 1965)

Pädagogischer Kongress (VII) der DDR (Staatsverlag, Berlin 1970)

Präzisierte Lehrpläne—all subjects (V u. W V, Berlin 1965)

Reinholdt, O. *Anleitung sum Einführungspraktikum an Instituten für Lehrerbildung* (Institut für Lehrerbildung, Halle/Saale 1970)

Richter, V. *Die Lehrerbildung in der DDR* (V u. W V, Berlin 1967)

Schönfelder, G. and Lost, G. *Zukunft von Anfang an* (Dietz, Berlin 1970)

Schwertner and Kempke. *Zur Wissenschafts u. Hochschulpolitik der SED* (V u. W V, 1967)

Sozialistisches Bildungsrecht (Staatsverlag, Berlin 1968)

Sozialistische Schule (Staatsverlag, Berlin 1964)

Statistisches Jahrbuch der DDR (Staatsverlag, Berlin 1970)

Subert, H. *Bildungspraxis in Deutschland* (Bertelmann Universitätsverlag, Düsseldorf 1970)

Reviews

Berufsbildung, 1968 (monthly, V u. W V, Berlin)

Bildungspläne in der BRD u. in der DDR (Schule u. Nation Verlag, GmbH, Schweln 1, Westf)

Elternhaus u. Schule (quarterly, V u. W V)

Das Hochschulwesen, 1952 (12 numbers a year until 1971: now 6 numbers)

Neue Erziehung im Kindergarten (quarterly, V u. W V)

Pädagogische Forschung (Ministry of Education, 6 numbers a year)

Pädagogik (quarterly, German Central Pedagogical Institute)

Polytechnische Bildung u. Erziehung, 1958 (monthly, German Central Pedagogical Institute, Berlin)

Vergleichende Pädagogik (quarterly, V u. W V, Berlin)

Index